SURVIVING AND PROSPERING IN THE SMALL FIRM SECTOR

The factors which determine the success or failure of small firms are complex and specific to this type of organization. Graham Hall draws on new empirical research to challenge some of the existing literature.

The book sheds light on the factors associated with the success and failure of small firms. Four of the chapters report new empirical studies, two on small firm failure, two on success. Other chapters review critically the state of knowledge on a diverse range of topics – age, size and failure, the efficiency of failure prediction models, owner characteristics and success, theories of strategy as they affect small firms, market-structure and small firms, including buyer power and franchising, and organization life cycles. The style of the book is very reader-friendly with a minimum of jargon and plentiful examples.

By exploring the influences which make or break a small company, this book will provide MBA students and business managers with important information about the probability of success or failure within organizations.

Graham Hall is Professor of Strategic Management at the University of Derby. This book was written whilst on the faculty of Manchester Business School.

SURVIVING AND PROSPERING IN THE SMALL FIRM SECTOR

Graham Hall

London and New York

First published 1995
by Routledge
11 New Fetter Lane, London EC4P 4EE

Simultaneously published in the USA and Canada
by Routledge
29 West 35th Street, New York, NY 10001

Typeset in Times by Michael Mepham, Frome, Somerset
Printed and bound in Great Britain by
TJ Press (Padstow) Ltd, Padstow, Cornwall

British Library Cataloguing in Publication Data
A catalogue record for this book is available
from the British Library

Library of Congress Cataloguing in Publication Data
Hall, Graham.
Surviving and prospering in the small
firm sector / Graham Hall.
p. cm.
Includes bibliographical references and index.
1. Small business—Management. 2. Small
business—Great Britain—Management. 3. Business
failures. 4. Business failures—Great Britain. I. Title.
HD2341.H27 1993
658.02'2—dc20

ISBN 0–415–07083–X (hbk)
ISBN 0–415–12806–4 (pbk)

CONTENTS

CONTENTS

TABLES

ACKNOWLEDGEMENTS

As is suggested by the acknowledgements within the text a cast of thousands has been involved in the research on which this book is based. My heartfelt thanks to them all. In addition I would like to express my gratitude to Jane Geddes who not only typed the text but made sure it made sense (or at least some sense) and to Marilyn, Ben and Tom for putting up (usually) with the strain of living with me over the long period when the book was written. Obviously, all mistakes are mine.

1

INTRODUCTION

The most likely reason why the owner of a small firm will attend a training course is to find out how she can maximize the chances of survival of her company and, if it survives, how she can achieve the highest possible level of success. She may be asked to read one of the several 'how to' books on the market, which usually concentrate on a narrow range of aspects of managing a small company, and are often based on a mixture of experience and the a priori reasoning of their authors as to what may be said to represent efficient management practices. The implication is that adoption of these practices will assist in ensuring survival and success.

This book is not intended to supply a set of prescriptions, though on occasions it does come close to doing so. Instead it has two aims. First, it reviews our state of knowledge about the factors which influence the probability of failure within the small-firm sector and affect the level of success among survivors. This review will encompass conclusions from empirical research and whatever theoretical frameworks are appropriate. Second, it reports the results of some new empirical studies on both failure and success.

Whereas it is to be hoped that the review is reasonably comprehensive, the choice of topics inevitably reflects the economics and strategy background of the author, though a foray was made (heroically or foolhardedly) into psychology's balliwick of owner personality. Otherwise, social scientists rather than economists may identify important influences on performance that have been omitted. Certainly, the literature on various non-strategic aspects of management will be largely ignored, except when comparing results with those suggested by the empirical studies reported here. The major omission was the effect of government policy, because this seemed too vast to be squeezed into a single chapter.

Within all of the management disciplines there is something of a stigma attached to being labelled a 'small firm expert'. Indeed, some significance may be drawn from a comment being made at all; an interest in large firms would normally go unremarked as though this were the natural field of study. The stigma is nowhere greater than in economics. Later chapters will show how economic theory has implications for the strategic management of small firms, but this was not usually the intention of its proponents.

A puzzle for historians of economic thought is why small firms have, indeed, been virtually ignored by economists. Theories are rarely formulated about their behaviour, samples rarely drawn from their populations. The very first micro-economic model with which students are normally confronted, perfect competition, consists entirely of small firms but is usually intended as a launching pad for understanding the large-firm sector, rather than to explain the operation of the small. The subtext of even the monopolistic competition model is more likely to be 'the implications of product differentiation in the absence of barriers to entry' rather than 'the market conditions facing many small firms', yet the second would be equally valid.

The puzzle arises from most firms being small. Well over ninety per cent have fewer than 100 employees, in fact many less, and collectively account for over two-thirds of output. Precise estimates are difficult to make for a number of reasons, not least the on-going revolution in employment practices in which permanent employees are replaced by the self-employed performing the same functions. Technically, the latter are one-person businesses with only a single customer, but for all intents and purposes, they are full or part-time employees, though without many of the safeguards that this status would normally imply. Though there is scope for disagreement about its extent, there would seem little doubt that the small-firm sector is more important than the large in both numbers and output.

An analogy may be drawn between the attitude of economists and, to a lesser extent, researchers from other management disciplines towards small firms, with the ignorance and indifference traditionally displayed by the British middle classes towards almost every aspect of working class life. The breathless accounts from the pre-war Mass Observation social surveys and the tone adopted by some post-war sociologists convey the impression that their subjects were some distant foreign tribe instead of the majority of British people.

Three of the empirical studies discussed in these pages use econometrics to identify the factors at least associated with and, very possibly, influencing the performance of three separate samples of small firms, where performance is variously defined as survival, profitability and growth. In so doing it is hoped that our knowledge of the small-firm sector will be modestly enhanced, which would seem laudible in its own right. A further reason is that studying small firms may provide insights into issues which surround large ones, analogous to biologists studying simple organisms in order to draw conclusions about more complex. Certainly large firms are characterized by complexity. It may prove possible for this to be unravelled with respect to individual firms through in-depth case studies. Replicating the studies reported in this book on a sample of large firms would probably not prove successful, however, because the sheer volume of factors which affect their performance could swamp the impact of individual, so that, at best, only the most important would be revealed statistically.

The small firm sector also provides the opportunity to draw much bigger samples than does the large. This improves the likelihood that the effects of individual factors will be isolated and measured and allows more factors to be held constant. The latter will prove important where interaction between factors might be expected. If the influence of a factor on the performance of a company is contingent, for example, on the structure of the market in which it operates, this interaction may possibly be taken into account explicitly in a statistical exercise. Otherwise, the sample must be drawn exclusively from the same market. This would clearly restrict sample sizes for large firms.

Given such compelling reasons for studying small firms one can only conjecture as to why they have been ignored by economists and, to some extent, by researchers in other management disciplines. Some issues, such as the exploitation of market power or interaction of business and politics, are almost certainly going to centre on large firms. The complexity of individual large firms may make them more interesting than small and speculating about the outcome of the battle between British Telecom and Mercury might provide greater excitement than between two high street solicitors. On the other hand, a more cynical reason might be that data is much more readily available about large firms. Indeed, it is possible to produce quite detailed cases, by the use of secondary sources, such as newspaper and market analyst reports, without ever going near the companies concerned. This has great significance for economists, who generally appear to exhibit a pathological reluctance, fortunately not shared by writers in other disciplines, about collecting information directly from the companies they are studying. When assembling data on individual small firms there is little alternative to communicating with the people who run them.

Over the last few years there has been an increased interest from economists in the small-firm sector and, indeed, in one very recent contribution, Gavin Reid (1993) has collected his data through personal interviews, making his work particularly path-breaking. Nevertheless, in terms of the volume of attention it has attracted, the small-firm sector remains the poor relation. Fortunately, sufficient has been written about issues which surround the economic and strategic management of small firms to be able to draw some reasonably clear conclusions or, at least, to be able to highlight the areas of controversy, even though writers may not claim to be economists, or even strategists. A significant proportion of those writing about small firms do not, in fact, have a background centring on a particular discipline, but developed an interest in researching small firms from training their owners.

Trainers form part of the intended readership of this book. It is to be hoped that academics and students with an interest in strategic issues in general, rather than those specializing in the strategic management of small firms, will also find it of some use. Because of this diverse catchment area, especially as regards knowledge of statistical methods, econometric results and technical jargon have been kept to a minimum. Where jargon is unavoidable its meaning would probably be familiar to most readers but, in any case, can be inferred from the context.

At this juncture some other definitions should perhaps be presented. 'Products' are used as shorthand for 'products or services'. Out of convenience 'owners' are assumed to be synonymous with 'principal decision-makers' though recognizing that, especially for the larger of the small firms, this may not always be warranted. Definitions of failure and success are both candidates for argument. This book will be rather insensitive as to what admittedly can represent an important controversy, particularly with regard to how the success of a small firm should be measured. In the empirical work reported 'failure' is defined as involuntary liquidation in one study, and involuntary cessation of business, in the other. In both cases there may have been some scope for interpretation as to the precise dates that failure occurred but not to the extent of appreciably altering the results. In the literature review of causes, failure is variously defined but, again, differences do not seem to make very much difference to the conclusions to be drawn. What does matter is the assumption in the two empirical studies of 'success' – that it can be measured by growth in sales or by profitability. It is hard to see how alternatives could have been employed in statistical analysis but this is certainly not to deny that growth and profitability are not the only objectives of owners of small firms. Others could easily be, for instance, the sense of freedom from being one's own boss, or the sense of achievement, or the sheer fun of running a business. In some cases 'hobby businesses' would be an accurate description. However, apart from the convenience of adopting simplistic definitions of success, growth and profitability, the latter in particular, will probably be at least important dimensions of performance, though this assertion may only reflect the economic inculcation of the author.

A further issue that will be ignored is how 'small' should be defined. The purposes of this book are best served by being eclectic, including in the review whatever seems relevant and useful, encompassing studies adopting various definitions. Usually, size is measured by numbers employed: up to ten, 100 (which is the most common), 200 or even 500, though the last is more often considered to be medium-sized. In the empirical studies reported in this book the samples were drawn from firms employing less than 100 in two cases, in fact usually much less, and less than 500 in a third case.

Adopting a fairly flexible view of what is meant by small has meant that pertinent studies have been included. This does not imply that researchers should be loose in the criteria by which they construct their sampling frames. It would seem certain that firms differing in size will also differ in other ways. One-man businesses probably do not exhibit identical characteristics to those of firms with ten employees, and firms with fifty are not the same as firms with 100 employees. The dimensions on which variation will occur, however, and the nature of the relationships, are largely a matter of conjecture. By the time a firm has reached a workforce of 100 it is very likely that some decision-making will be delegated by owners to professional managers, but what is less obvious is in what other respects the firms will change with this growth, or what will happen if the workforce is then doubled or trebled. There is a literature on organization life-cycles, which will be discussed later, but, even if its stages are quite distinct, and related to size rather than, say, age, the range of factors included in organization lifecycle models is fairly limited.

This ignorance about the changes that accompany growth make it advisable for sampling frames to be defined tightly in terms of both lower and upper limits. This has nothing to do with defining 'small' as any definition will be arbitrary, but it is a recognition that size may be a factor which affects the influences of variables being considered.

Some justification should be made about the methodology employed in three of the reported empirical studies. Because of the number of variables encompassed and the lack of any strong theory regarding their relative importance, this was determined by various step-wise procedures. These have definite weaknesses which have rendered such procedures an anathema to many economists. It is hoped, in fact, that the safeguards adopted have avoided, at least, the most damaging of these weaknesses, but the instinct of readers with economics backgrounds will probably remain that it is far more valid to test a specific model than to infer the most important influences on performance from the strength of statistical relationships.

The results may, however, give economists some cause for reflection on their methodology. It seems that many diverse factors can affect performance. Choosing a particular set, and ignoring all others, requires a strong faith in one's theory. This is a general observation about all issues in economics but, to take performance as an example, if the sort of factors that appear to affect the performance of small firms also affect that of large, the reliability of the results from the vast market-structure company performance literature will, to some extent, be brought into question. The assumption that all other influences on performance are completely independent of market-structure may be quite valid but must remain an act of faith until subjected to empirical examination.

The structure of this book reflects its twin aims: to review the state of knowledge on the reasons for failure and success among small firms, and to present the results of new studies on these topics.

Chapter 2 discusses why failure is concentrated among firms that are small and young, presenting three quite separate sets of explanations.

Chapter 3 considers the evidence on which small firms are likely to fail, paying particular attention to the conclusions to be drawn from predictive models.

Chapter 4 assesses the information supplied on involuntary insolvency by the reports from the Official Receiver, with particular regard to the opinions of owners as to why their companies failed.

Chapter 5 presents the results of an empirical study of reasons for failure among small firms, drawing its sample from the UK construction sector.

Chapter 6 opens the discussion of factors influencing the success of small firms by considering what might be said about the importance of owner personality.

Chapter 7 pays some attention to the impact of formal strategic planning on performance.

Chapter 8 attempts to show how quite basic micro-economic theory has strong implications for the strategies that should be pursued by small firms.

Chapter 9 discusses how market structure might affect a small firm's performance, focusing on franchising, which could well be a manifestation of supplier power and on changing developments in relationships with customers.

Chapter 10 considers the evidence on the existence of organization life-cycles, frequently regarded as important in the literature on small firms.

Chapter 11 discusses the relative importance of various influences on performance, as suggested by a new study based on the UK instrumentation sector.

Chapter 12 presents the results of an international comparison of the influences on the performance of small firms.

Finally, Chapter 13 tries to make sense of what has gone before and to draw some conclusions about the policies that might be adopted by both small firms and by the government.

2

PERFORMANCE, SIZE AND AGE

There is no doubt that the probability of a company's survival increases positively with:

- its size
- its age.

To quote from Evans (1987a):

> At the sample mean, a 1 per cent change in firm size leads to a seven per cent change in the probability of survival; a one per cent change in age leads to a 13 per cent change in the probability of survival. The positive coefficient on the product of size and age implies that the probability of survival increases with size more rapidly for older firms and that the probability of survival increases with age more rapidly for larger firms.

Even modest changes in size can increase the chances of survival. The following, extracted from Phillips and Kirchhoff (1989), shows the proportion of companies in each growth category that survived to 1984–86 from being started in 1976–78:

Absolute growth in employees:

0	1–4	5–9	10+	all classes
26.0	65.0	75.6	77.2	37.2

These studies draw their samples from populations of American small firms but the thrust of their results would not be inconsistent with those of Ganguly (1985), on the breakdown by size and age of UK companies deregistering for Value Added Tax, or of Hudson (1987) on the distribution of ages of the various kinds of British liquidations.

This chapter will consider three explanations for the negative relationship between the probability of a firm failing and its size, all of which have some degree of relevance for the negative age–failure relationship.

These explanations should be regarded as complimentary, rather than as alternatives. They centre on:

- The Jovanovic model.
- The implications of the limited portfolios represented by small firms.
- The relationship of market structure to failure among small firms.

Before doing so, however, some reference should be made to the relationship of size to another measure of performance, growth. A celebrated theory, usually termed Gibrat's Law, hypothesizes that average growth rates are independent of firm size. This has been subject to extensive empirical testing. Here, attention will be limited to two recent studies based on small American firms or on plants.

Evans (1987b) found that growth decreased with firm size for eighty-nine out of 100 industries. Dunne, Roberts and Samuelson (1989), when considering the growth patterns of plants, found that the mean growth rate of survivors declined with size and with age. For single-plant firms, the growth rates were negative in the larger classes, but for multi-plant firms they were positive. When failures and survivors were pooled, single-plant firms (the experience of which would have most relevance for the purposes of this book), suffered a decline in growth with size, as the decline overwhelmed the effects of a reduction in the failure rate. The effect of age is less clear as growth rates apparently declined with age for the small-sized group but then increased and declined for larger plants. Interestingly, this pattern differed from that of multi-plant firms. For those that were young the relationship was U-shaped with growth rates declining with size for plants with less than 100 employees and increasing with size for plants with over 100. For plants over five years old mean growth rates increased with plant size. This is because the effect of the reduction in the failure rate overwhelmed the effect of the reduction in the growth rate of surviving plants.

THE JOVANOVIC MODEL

Economists have had surprisingly little to say about corporate failure but a notable exception is represented by Jovanovic (1982), whose contribution truly deserves to be described as seminal. The mathematics would be too impenetrable for most readers but a more user-friendly translation is provided by Dunne, Roberts and Samuelson (*op. cit.*). The idea behind the model is relatively simple, though this is in no way to disparage the value of the insights that it provides.

Firms are assumed to make output decisions based on their efficiency levels but to be unaware of what these levels actually are. Instead, they are depicted as being faced with a probability distribution of possible cost levels from which they draw over successive periods. Over time they learn more about their efficiency. Those that are most efficient, enjoying the lowest costs, expand their output. Those that are least efficient contract and, if their output falls below a specific level, 'the failure boundary' as coined by Dunne, Roberts and Samuelson (*op. cit.*) they will cease to produce altogether. This process can be expressed as a critical growth path. If this is not maintained, exit will occur.

Jovanovic (1982) draws an impressively long series of conclusions from this model but of relevance to this chapter are:

- Differences in firm size would reflect different positions along the critical growth path. The larger a firm the less likely that it will be taken by surprise by unfavourable cost levels and find its optimal output to lie below the failure boundary. Hence the positive relationship between size and the probability of survival.
- Older firms would have had more time to learn about their costs, and so will have more accurate estimates of their costs. Again unpleasant surprises in their costs, and concomitant future output levels, will prove less likely as the firm gains in age.

The learning that occurs in the Jovanovic model reduces the ignorance about costs but does not reduce the level of costs in a manner usually associated with learning curves. The latter do have a role to play, however. As Bates (1990) points out, previous knowledge of running a business could lower the degree of uncertainty about costs and speed progress along the critical growth path. Possibly other forms of human capital, for instance resulting from higher education, may have a similar effect, not only in increasing efficiency but in providing a clearer picture of what the efficiency level might actually be. That will be the premise in the empirical study of failure in the construction industry the results of which will be discussed in Chapter 5.

SMALL FIRMS AS LIMITED PORTFOLIOS

This section proposes a fresh explanation for the concentration of failure among small firms. This is that, in two quite distinct ways, small firms represent limited portfolios, each of which may affect both their level of earnings and variability of earnings over time.

The first concerns the opportunities open to small firms. These take the form of the products they offer and the markets in which they operate. Both products and markets represent a potential stream of earnings and, collectively, may be regarded as a portfolio of assets in much the same way as the more conventionally termed portfolio of financial assets. But their features will be likely to differ, however. Product-market portfolios will be far more susceptible than financial to economies of scale and of scope.

Economies of scale represent the advantages from size. In markets where these are strong small firms must limit their attention to particular niches. These can be carved out because of an absence of scale economies, a lack of demand to warrant the exploitation of such economies even if they do potentially exist, or because of the advantages of specialization. The first and last of these would not explain why large firms are not serving these niches. In principle, in the absence of such impediments to perfect competition as patents, and the preferences of people with unique skills to be their own boss, there is very little that small firms can do that cannot be achieved by large. To be sure, the decision-making process within large firms may reduce their flexibility to meet the needs of a multitude of individual and limited markets but this can be remedied by sub-dividing into units that are quasi-autonomous. Analogously, many battles can be fought by armies directed from central command posts, or by bands of guerrillas with minimal direction from above. In short, small firms have less opportunities than large and, even in the markets in which they do operate, enjoy freedom from harassment by large firms only for as long as the latter are constrained by their organizational structure or by the low returns from these markets.

Economies of scope represent the advantages from offering particular combinations of products or from operating in particular combinations of markets (Panzar and Willig, 1975; Teece, 1980). Normally the assumption behind financial portfolio theory is that investment is made sequentially in assets with diminishing levels of expected future earnings. Hence, as the riskiness of the portfolio diminishes as it increases in size so does its average return, producing the familiar risk–return trade-off. An effect of economies of scope is to remove this trade-off with respect to product-market portfolios.

The possibility of producing a range of products on the same

11

production facilities; excess capacity in the transport of something different; knowledge gained in one market being put to good use in another; even the competitive advantage provided to new products from trading under an established brand-name, are all examples of economies of scope. They can mean that as the breadth of the product-market portfolio is increased its average return also rises, producing the opposite of the risk–return trade-off.

Economies of scale will, therefore, limit the opportunities open to small firms and economies of scope may mean that large firms are able to enjoy the best of all worlds; the lower risk from a bigger portfolio of products and markets, with a higher return. Little wonder, therefore, that small firms are more vulnerable to failure than large ones.

Matters are, however, made much worse by the second way in which small firms represent limited portfolios, that is in the volume of managerial skills at their disposal. On average, the level of managerial expertise of a manager in a small firm is lower than in a large. It is probably the case that the remuneration to all types of workers, especially managers,[1] is on average lower in the small firm sector which must have some implications for the quality of staff they recruit. Certainly graduates are more likely to be attracted to large firms – though the popularity in the UK of graduate enterprise schemes which are intended to train graduates to become self-employed, would suggest this is less and less the case – as are people with formal management education, such as MBAs. Bigger companies are also more likely to provide in-house training or to sponsor attendance on management courses and, just as important, to offer the opportunity to employ state of the art techniques.

It would be quite invalid, of course, indeed ridiculous to argue that the level of managerial talent will invariably be lower in a small firm. Apart from the possibility that managers may develop their skills within a large firm before moving into the small-firm sector, there is much more to the art of management than might be suggested by levels of academic achievement or knowledge of management techniques. Being able to identify opportunities in the absence of hard data and to exploit these opportunities effectively; being able to display creativity, and being willing to back one's intuition with more than one can afford to lose are not attributes which can readily be taught or which are associated with levels of formal education. It could, indeed, easily be argued that people with these skills would be more willing to start, or work for, small firms operating in those sectors where they would be of the greatest value – fashion clothing, for instance, rather than a firm of solicitors – than to join a large firm, the culture of which might discourage entrepreneurialism.

However talented she may be, the smaller the firm in which a manager must operate, the greater the range of skills that she is required to display. The owner–manager of a very small firm may need to make decisions across the full range of management disciplines, with support from her accountant and advice from her bank manager. As firms grow in size they are able to increase their number of specialist managers but the degree of specialization that is viable is clearly an important facet of economies of scale which increases the disadvantage faced by small firms.

It is not just a matter of being able to call on managers with skills in various disciplines. The more limited the volume of managerial talent available to a firm the more limited the range of situations which its management team can effectively confront or exploit. The management team of a recently founded company, for instance, may possess the skills necessary to spot an untapped niche in a market, estimate its size, convince a bank manager of its viability and to install an information control system adequate to meet its needs. The same team may not possess the skills to successfully manage the problems of control that arise with growth (Ray and Hutchinson, 1983) or to meet the challenge from new competition.

The most appropriate skills may vary with the stages of growth through which a company passes or with the characteristics of its markets. They may also vary with stages in economic or cultural environments. Casual empiricism suggests a decline in demand from major UK business schools for courses on man-management, in particular industrial relations, and an increase in demand for courses on managing change and on environmental issues.

Further, instability may arise in the personal circumstances of the management team. One effect of the lack of depth in the team is that any factor which may prove detrimental to the competence of one or more of its members – serious illness, divorce, bereavement – may jeopardise the survival of a firm to an extent that would never be expected in a large firm with its greater scope for providing back-up.

FAILURE AND MARKET STRUCTURE

Though this would not appear to have been remarked upon by writers on small firm failure (perhaps because of its self-evidence!) but the markets which are characterized by populations of small firms are likely to experience a high rate of failure. In those markets or, more commonly, segments of markets, in which competition is achieved primarily on the basis of price, the size of the population of firms will be determined by the relationship of the output of firms to their costs and by the total volume of output. The size of this population will reflect the number of firms that can simultaneously achieve the minimum efficient scale, the level of output at which most of the advantages from size have been exhausted. If all firms shared the same minimum efficient scale and if this represented, say, one-hundredth of the market's output, other things remaining equal, the population would consist of 100 firms.

This simple picture is confused by economies of scope, the advantages from offering a range of products. These advantages will vary with the ranges offered. For example, a manufacturer of female clothing may be able to exploit the excess capacity in his resources, especially capital equipment, to achieve the minimum efficient scale in male clothing at a lower level of output than if he had entered the clothing business for the first time. Hence, the minimum efficient scale that a company must attain in the output of a product in order to benefit from lowest possible cost levels will depend upon the combination of other products that it produces.

By definition, small firms are denied the opportunity to benefit from economies of scale. They will usually be offered little alternative to operating in markets in which the minimum efficient scale is achieved at low levels of output and the number of firms is correspondingly high. They may be able to compensate with economies of scope for their lack of size and, therefore, to occupy segments of markets normally occupied by large companies, but examples where the potential for such compensation is substantial, are fairly rare and, where there are exceptions, the pertinent question then centres on the factors preventing other firms of similar size producing the same range of products.

If such factors are not difficult to achieve the result for small firms will be the same as if there had been an absence of economies of scope. They may run the distinct risk of operating in a segment that will become overcrowded, the level of overall demand proving insufficient to support all of the firms that wish to operate in it.

The volume of sales that any firm will earn will be determined by the total level of demand within its segment and its share of that level. A firm calculating the benefits from entering a market must, therefore, make two separate predictions. Unfortunately, estimating likely market-share implies taking into account not only the number of current operators and their likely reaction to new entrants but similar considerations regarding potential entrants. Firms must second-guess the decisions of potential entrants and try to envisage what the market will be likely to be like after their entry.

Such calculations made by large firms form meaty topics within the pages of strategy case books. There are, after all, only a limited number of companies that, for instance, could operate in telecommunications and their probable behaviour can clearly fruitfully be subject to, at least, the educated speculation of business strategists, even if some of the techniques suggested by modern game theorists verge on the fanciful!

Small firms are not usually afforded the luxury of only a few potential entrants to their markets. If a market appears attractive to an owner of a small firm she will be painfully aware not only that others are making a similar assessment but that just how many will be uncertain, and this uncertainty will increase the lower the economies of scale. It is certainly no coincidence that successive *Yellow Pages* can give the impression of transitions from famines to feasts; one year there may be a handful of taxi firms, hairdressers or private security firms, the next year consumers may be spoilt for choice.

So far the discussion has centred on the implications of low economies of scale for potential market entrants. They would not be very different for incumbent firms. They face the very real possibility that their segments will become overcrowded. The volume of failures that will result will depend upon the height of barriers to exit around the segment. The nature of these barriers will be discussed in Chapter 9. Suffice to say here that if it is difficult to respond to overcrowding by moving elsewhere failures will be inevitable.

It is easy to write condescendingly about the naivety displayed by the owners of small firms finding themselves the victims of overcrowding but it is hard to see how this can be avoided if they are not in a position to operate in a market surrounded by a non-scale barrier to entry. Although economies of scale represents the most potent barrier, there are, fortunately, others and the markets they encompass are likely to suffer lower failure rates than markets without any significant barriers. As will be discussed in Chapter 8, knowledge, broadly defined, represents one such barrier, and it is possible to think in terms of the minimum efficient level of knowledge necessary to operate in a market, the implications of which would be similar to those of the minimum efficient scale of other factors of production.

For example, it does not take as long to build up sufficient knowledge, i.e. human capital, to become a house decorator as would be required to be a lawyer. Not surprisingly the failure rate among law firms is lower than within the decorating business.

As an alternative to operating in a market surrounded by non-scale barriers to entry a firm may choose to occupy a niche in which there is insufficient demand to sustain more than a few firms. Ideally, indeed, it should operate in a niche which is sufficiently large to provide a healthy return for one firm but not two. Such strategies are most common where the niches are geographical. In the suburbs of Manchester, UK, in which the author lives, for instance, there is a sufficiently large Jewish population to justify one kosher butcher but no more, and this fact appears to be obvious to other butchers with the potential to supply this highly specialist market. That is not to say, of course, that another kosher butcher may not, at some time in the future, set up in competition in the area, either because of over-optimism in his estimate of the size of the market or because of a belief that he would prove the survivor in the ensuing competition.

FAILURE AND CORPORATE AGE

Whilst the Jovanovic model explicitly offers an explanation for the reduced probability of failure with increases in corporate size and age, the last two sections are mostly concerned with the former. They do, however, have some implications for the relationship of failure to age. Their portfolios of product markets may not provide sufficient return to warrant staying in business or may be too limited to facilitate adequate economies of scope. Owners are likely to be aware of either fairly early after starting their business and, in the absence of alternative activities, or in the hope of matters improving, will limp on until their capital is exhausted. This is fairly obviously not so much a case, as in the Jovanovic model, of owners learning about their efficiency, important as this will be, as about the state of demand for their products and potential for economies of scope.

Less obvious is the relationship of age to the portfolio of managerial skills within a firm. The longer a firm survives, the greater the range of problems with which it will be buffeted. Over time its management will meet increasingly less fresh problems and will be able to draw on experience to meet successive threats. The longer the period that elapses the less likely that such threats will not have been confronted

16

before. Hence, the longer its track record, the longer a firm is likely to stay in business in the future.

Barriers to entry will also affect the age at which firms fail. Low barriers imply fast overcrowding within a market. Dunne, Roberts and Samuelson (1988) found a correlation between the volume of entry above average for a sector in one period to be correlated with the above-average volume of exits in the following period. The length of these periods was five years.

CONCLUDING REMARKS

The probability of a firm failing falls as it increases in size and as it increases in age. This is one of the most striking features of the statistics on corporate death. There is unlikely to be a single overriding explanation for such a strong relationship. This chapter has discussed three sets of explanations: the Jovanovic model; the limited portfolio (both in management skills and product-markets) represented by small firms; and the effect of low barriers to entry. Probably they each have a part to play.

3

WHICH SMALL FIRMS FAIL?

Understanding the reasons for the inverse correlation between firm size and likelihood of failure provides only limited insight into the factors distinguishing failures from survivors, especially if they face market conditions that are broadly similar. Jovanovic's (1982) model predicts that failure would be less probable in the presence of variables, suggesting that progress along a managerial learning curve either has already been achieved or could be achieved more readily. Such variables might be levels of education and management experience. Bates' (1990) empirical study provided mixed support for Jovanovic. The theory linking small-firm failures to their limited portfolio of managerial skills leads us to expect that firms fail for different reasons at different stages of their development, a prediction confirmed by the evidence presented in the next chapter, and that failure will become less likely with the increase in the size of the portfolio. The latter arises if the skill levels of individual managers is enhanced, consistent with Jovanovic's model, or if the disciplines encompassed by the management team are expanded, which would not be inconsistent with Jovanovic, and certainly would be a further explanation for the positive relationship between the size of a firm and its probability of survival.

The literature that might further our understanding of why some small firms fail while others survive may be divided into:

- Direct address of the issue of what constitutes efficiency, where efficiency is here defined as adopting management practices which minimize the likelihood of failure.
- Indirect address, through the construction of prediction models of failure.

18

- Studies of factors influencing differences in the total volume of failures over time.

REASONS FOR FAILURE

The most well-known set of reasons has been presented by Argenti (1976). These are:

- One-man rule by chief executives who 'dominate their colleagues rather than lead them, who make decisions in spite of their hostility or reticence'.
- A non-participating board, which reinforces one-man rule.
- An 'unbalanced top team', with respect to its skill-base.
- A weak finance function, described as a 'special case of imbalance in the top team'.
- Lack of management depth, though Argenti does not appear to feel very strongly about this.
- The combination of chairman and chief executive roles in a single person, because otherwise there is no-one above the latter to 'shake him awake or direct him or warn him or dismiss him'. This Argenti describes as the 'most important defect'.

Argenti goes on to argue that companies suffering from these weaknesses will be likely to employ poor financial information, will respond badly to change and may well overtrade, launch a single project that is dangerously big, or will allow their gearing to rise to levels that convert 'normal business hazards' into 'constant threats'.

Though Argenti is not particularly concerned to make this point, many of the weaknesses he describes are particularly prevalent among small firms. The smaller the enterprise the more likely that it will be run by one person (though whether it is fair to describe this as 'autocratic' is another matter); that it will not have so much a non-participating as a non-existent board; that its management team will be both imbalanced and lacking in depth; that its financial system will be poor; and that it will be tempted, perhaps from lack of choice, into investing in a project too big for its own resources.

Argenti based his theory on the evidence from a few cases of failure among big firms. Some of his hypotheses are tested on a large sample of small firms by Storey, Keasey, Watson and Wynarczk (1987). The results of this are included below in the discussion of the prediction literature.

Argenti presents a set of cogent arguments as to why corporate failure occurs, albeit unsupported by hard evidence. If the extreme view is adopted that the prediction literature is not relevant, surprisingly few other writers have attempted any level of explanation. Berryman (1983), in her admirably conscientious trawl of the literature, is not able to identify very many and none that might accurately be described as being elevated to the status of a standard source. One reason for this might be that writers may simply be drawing on their experience for their opinions, for instance Hartigan (1976) as an insolvency practitioner. Naturally, these opinions could be perfectly well-founded but, in the absence of hard data, there is no way of knowing. Where a sample of failures is employed it is usually in the absence of a control group of survivors. This criticism might be levied at Larson and Clute (1979), who base their conclusions on the records of 359 small businesses that had approached the American Small Business Administration for help with severe financial difficulties.[1] Without a control group it is not possible to state with any certainty that the characteristics of the firms experiencing such difficulties were not shared by more successful firms facing similar conditions.

Furthermore, where there is a control group, as is implied by Litvak and Maule (1980) in their longitudinal study of the fates of new technologically orientated Canadian companies, scientific methods are not applied to identify the differences between survivors and failures. In the absence of the sort of methods commonly employed in the construction of prediction models, it is usually not possible to identify accurately which of many factors are important and which are not.[2]

If all the reservations about methodology are laid aside can any conclusions be drawn from the literature which explicitly attempts to provide reasons for corporate failure? If there were a consensus as to the nature of the reasons that certainly might be highly significant but this is singularly lacking, with each writer seemingly putting the blame on a different factor or, rather, set of factors. Indeed, Litvak and Maule (op. cit.) are unusual in focusing on a particular aspect of management, in this case unrealistic expectations by founders as to the initial returns from their businesses.

Other writers do not feel able to be quite so specific. Hartigan (op. cit.) cites as reasons for failure: inadequate capital; poor costing; lack of management control; 'imprudent business judgement'; a set of 'general economic factors' which is itself fairly diverse; fraud, and inability by the founder to manage a growing company. Kamal and

Hughey (1977) produce a similarly long list of aspects of management that they believe are important to the survival of a small business: credit planning; cash management; personnel policy; bookkeeping; merchandising and tax planning, as do Larson and Clute (op. cit.) in their catalogue of owner characteristics, and various areas of marketing and financial planning. In short, if owners were to be effective at all of the elements of running a firm considered by one or other of these writers to be important it would seem safe to conclude they could not but be successful.

PREDICTING FAILURE

Until the 1980s virtually all of the literature on corporate failure dealt with whether it could be predicted. It is usually dated from the pioneering work by Beaver (1967; 1968) and Altman (1968) and, though since then the literature has grown too vast to do it full justice, noteworthy contributions have been made by Deakin (1977), Blum (1974) and Ohlson (1980) using American data and Taffler (1982) using British. Useful surveys are supplied by Zavgren (1983), Taffler (1983) and Altman (1984) and an excellent evaluation of the accuracy of some of the models is provided by Hamer (1983). Samples are almost invariably drawn from the large, usually quoted, sector with exceptions represented by Edmister (1972) and the seminal work by Storey, Keasey, Watson and Wynarczk (1987), and associated papers by members of this team. Data usually comprises financial ratios, derived from published accounts, on a sample of firms that have failed and a control group of survivors, sometimes matched in some way. The methods employed to analyse this data vary from simple comparisons of averages through to multivariate discriminate analysis and qualitative response models. The more sophisticated the methodology, the more that can be inferred about the change in the probability of failure associated with a change in the level of any particular variable.

As the purpose of this book is to discuss the reasons for corporate failure, with particular reference to small firms, it is not necessary to undertake a comprehensive evaluation of the prediction models. A damaging critique of their usefulness has, however, been mounted by Wood and Piesse (1988), in particular with respect to the costs and benefits of their use even assuming their accuracy to be as high as their authors commonly claim. The most telling of Wood and Piesse's points refer to the underestimate of profits foregone by not investing in companies predicted to fail which, in fact, survive.

As far as aiding our understanding of the reasons for failure, the following should be noted.

Levels of ratios

What is not made explicit is why any of the variables, individually or collectively, are expected to make any difference to the probability of failure by a particular firm. It is not merely that choice of variables is hardly ever justified theoretically, to which a return will be made below, but that, rather more fundamentally, it is not clear why any of the variables are expected to be important.

There are two reasons why they might be. First, they might serve as warning signals of irretrievable unprofitability[3] in the not too distant future. In this case prediction models will serve the useful purpose of enabling the capital market to spot the potential survivors in which to invest, and to avoid the potential failures. Second, prediction models might be reflecting the decision-making process taking place within the capital market regardless of whether statistical techniques were employed and regardless of whether this process is actually leading to the right investment decisions being made. Quite clearly, if all decision-makers within the capital market – the most relevant of which for small firms will usually be bank managers – were to employ the same prediction model, a firm predicted to fail would find it impossible to raise fresh capital and, in consequence, probably would fail; the prophecy would be self-fulfilling. Even in the absence of any formal or explicit model, however, suppose that the consensus within the capital market was that a specific level of a particular variable was dangerously low (as with sales/assets ratios) or high (as with debt/equity ratios). Firms not achieving (or surpassing, as appropriate) these ratios would be likely to fail, irrespective of whether this cut-off ratio indeed provided an accurate barometer of future profitability.

It is important to remember that there is no theoretical reason why any ratio should have a specific value associated with survival or failure. What might be expected, however, is that in the early stages of a project, for instance the launch of a new product, cashflow will be negative, the ratio of sales to assets will be low and all the other ratios will appear similarly unhealthy. It is not unknown even for large firms to attempt to implement a strategy which initially has detrimental effects, reflected in apparently unfavourable financial ratios. Small firms, with their limited portfolios of product markets, certainly face the possibility of such unfavourable ratios at sometime in their lives. The evidence suggests that a reason for the high incidence of failure among small independent businesses may be that bank managers adopt more stringent criteria regarding what is an acceptable level of a particular ratio, or the length of time that a specific level is deemed unacceptable, than is adopted by the capital markets internal to large firms in their allocation of funds between their constituent businesses (Biggadike, 1979).

To take this line of argument to its extreme, perhaps somewhat unfairly, at best prediction models are merely reflecting an efficient decision-making process but are redundant as tools to help that process, though they may serve to aid our understanding of its operation. At worst, they are.providing an academic respectability to a process that is inefficient at spotting the truly profitable.

To the extent that some of the models discussed in the literature are commercially available their authors presumably believe that what they are offering represents an improvement on the tools otherwise available to the capital market when making its evaluation of future profitability and certainly this is the tone of the great majority of papers in this area. At the same time, however, authors are often at pains to stress the familiarity of the measures they employ to the capital market, specifically banks, with Beaver (1968) stating that the purpose of his study was to 'empirically evaluate alternative accounting measures', implying that they were currently being employed.

Prediction models may include the variables on which banks base their investment decisions but may achieve a more accurate estimation of their relationship to the probability of failure. Evidence of the efficiency with which banks use financial ratios has been derived from experiments rather than direct observation of how the people with responsibility for the lending decision actually make real-life decisions. In these experiments, loan officers – the data is for the most part American-based – are provided with financial profiles of companies, consisting of failures and survivors, and asked to categorize the sample into the two groups.

Libby (1975) in his meticulous study finds that loan officers were able to achieve results that were better than if they had based their decisions purely on chance. Casey (1980) finds rather less accuracy, especially as regards the categorization of failures. This might be explained by his withholding information on the ratio of failures to survivors, though in doing so he is perhaps applying a bigger handicap than banks would normally face when carrying out their business. In practice they probably have a fairly good idea of survival rates (though it may be argued that if they were more optimistic they would be encouraged to make loans to companies that would otherwise fail for lack of capital, producing a virtuous circle of self-fulfilment). Interestingly, Casey draws on Jung's theories to generate the hypothesis, which his results would appear to confirm, that 'intuitors', who take a more holistic approach, would be more likely to be successful than 'sensors', who focus on isolated details. Implicitly, this would seem a rationale for model-building, even if the importance of variables is determined intuitively, rather than through the application of statistical techniques. Kennedy (1975) is less clear than Libby (op. cit.) or Casey (op. cit.) on the conclusions to be drawn about the effectiveness with which loan officers use financial information but did suggest the importance of other types of information, such as outside credit ratings. Zimmer (1986), when studying the decision-making processes of Australian loan officers, produces results more consistent with those of Libby than Casey, though he did not find the officers performed much better with the data than a sample of part-time students!

When British trade credit specialists were provided with similar information by Keasey and Watson (1986) they performed no better than if their decisions had been taken randomly. However, this study went a step further than the others discussed here by comparing the efficiency of the specialists with that of a statistical model. The latter just about improved on randomness.

Lessons about failure

Only a limited amount can be inferred from prediction models about the reasons for company failure. Partly this results from the lack of insight provided by financial data. Obviously, knowing that firms that fail have a history of losses is not particularly revelatory and, to varying degrees, all of the various ratios derivable from published accounts are similarly only symptoms of whatever has been happening within a firm. Heavy borrowing by a firm destined to fail, for instance, may represent a desperate last-ditch attempt to cover costs or, conversely, may demonstrate an optimism about the future, later shown to be unwarranted.

The other reason why prediction models are not very helpful in assisting our understanding of the factors underlying failure is that they were never intended to do so. For the purposes of most of the studies employing such models it is only necessary that variables be identified which collectively produce predictions of failure that remain reliable over time and between samples, which minimize the twin dangers of investing in failures and missing the opportunity to invest in firms that would have survived, and which prove more accurate than alternative methods, the judgement of credit assessors for instance. Hence, it is not unusual for variables to be selected by purely statistical criteria. Taffler (1982), for instance, started his exploration of the data with forty-eight ratios derived from profit and loss accounts and balance sheets, forty-eight from funds statements and forty-four from year trend variables. After applying state of the art techniques he concluded that firms were more likely to fail if they had been unprofitable and had a high level of liabilities and that these are more important than the more short-run measures of working capital and speed of stockturn.

Whereas this is undoubtedly helpful a broader view of the process of failure might have been achieved if that had been the aim of Taffler's study and the same can be said of the prediction literature in general.

Although occasional studies may have included variables designed to reflect the long term or the degree of volatility of data, conclusions cannot readily be drawn about the length of time problems are experienced by failed firms, their apparent consistency over time and the nature of the inter-relationships between financial variables. It is, therefore, not straightforward to establish the degree to which failure results from fatal underlying weaknesses or sudden catastrophes (though, admittedly, the predictive power of models based on data for four or five years before failure would lend more weight to the former) nor to identify which groups of variables always seem to arise together nor, for that matter, whether there are such groups.

The most comprehensive picture so far of the factors associated with failure has been provided by Storey et al. (op. cit.) with, for the purposes of this book, the decidedly added bonus that their samples of survivors and failures were drawn from the small-firm sector. Although their study is principally concerned with the prediction of failure it provides many insights into why some small firms survive while others fail. Its data is very comprehensive and it employs non-financial variables in its model building.

When the values for the financial variables are averaged across firms:

- Failures have lower returns than survivors but do not necessarily have a history of losses. In two of the seven years encompassed by the study failed companies, on average, were making pre-tax profits two years before failure and, after tax and before depreciation, profits for four of the years. Indeed, whereas 68 per cent of all the failures were making losses after allowance for tax and depreciation two years before failure, as opposed to 36 per cent of survivors, these figures fell to 47 per cent and 19 per cent, respectively, after tax and before depreciation. In other words, if one does not adopt what most economists would regard as the rather irrational accounting convention of arbitrarily distributing over time the costs of plant and machinery, over half of the firms destined to fail were making profits as near to failure as two years before. Over half were making pre-tax profits, even if depreciation is deducted, three, four and five years before failure, and if depreciation is not deducted, only about a quarter were making losses five years before failure, and approximately one-third four and three years before. Hence, though failures do not have a history of doing as well as survivors, it would seem that whatever caused their demise, albeit perhaps representing the final straw, occurred in only the last three years of their corporate life, and this conclusion would be drawn, whatever the measure of profitability adopted. In terms of what is arguably the most appropriate measure, profits were being made as recently as two years before failure. Unfortunately, the strength of the conclusions that can be drawn is somewhat diluted by the sample apparently including firms in the first two or three years of their life.
- When attention is focused on the twenty-five failures that survived at least seven years, it does not appear that they usually experienced a steady decline in profitability, confirming the last point above. They would appear, however, to have experienced greater volatility over time in their profitability than a control group of survivors. Either from mismanagement, or from conditions external to their firms, it would appear that levels of sales and/or costs were far more erratic for failures than for survivors.
- Although it must be emphasized that nothing can be inferred about causation it appeared that failed firms borrowed more than survivors with the differences increasing as failure approached. There was, however, great variation between failures in the amount that they borrowed.
- Whilst, the problems that cause, or at least precipitate, failure may

be essentially short-run, in the absence of an economically rational banking system, measures designed to reflect the ability of firms to meet their immediate obligations, the ratios of net working capital to fixed assets and of current assets to current liabilities, did not appear to be very helpful in distinguishing between survivors and failures.The distribution (i.e. number within each sample taking each value) of these ratios displayed too much overlap to conclude that failed companies were more insolvent or illiquid than survivors, but this certainly does not mean that failure did not occur because of insolvency or illiquidity, only that some firms might have been better able than others to deal with these types of problems. The overlap between the distribution of values of the financial statistics taken by survivors and failures is the probable reason why they were not apparently statistically significant in the predictive models of failure Storey *et al.* (op. cit.)tried to construct. The latter, however, proved successful when they introduced variables either directly suggested by Argenti (op. cit.) to be important, e.g. the number of directors or indirectly suggested, e.g. the delay between audits and submission of accounts, or qualifications by auditors of current accounts, as an indication that the owners had indulged in creative accounting. Interestingly, qualifications on the accounts of companies on which qualifications had been previously expressed did not appear to make any difference, implying that what should be regarded as cause for concern is not a history of creative accounting but rather whether such behaviour is unusual.

INFLUENCES ON THE AGGREGATE NUMBER OF FAILURES

Over time the number of business failures will vary. It would be helpful to know the factors that were most important in determining this number because, by implication, the failures had proved unsuccessful at managing them. Only in the gloomiest scenarios would small firms be offered no scope for determining their own fate with whether they succumbed to falls in the level of demand for their products, or exogenously determined increases in their costs, being purely a matter of luck in this case. The quality of management would be constant across firms. This would seem an unlikely proposition which would, of course, render books like this quite irrelevant.

Surprisingly, little would appear to have been written in this area. Wadhwani (1986), in an influential paper, examines the effect of inflation on the incidence of compulsory and creditors' voluntary liquidations.[4] His starting point is that, in an imperfect capital market, inflation can influence the volume of corporate failures by its disproportionate effect upon the value of interest repayments. One cannot improve on his example:

> Suppose that the real interest rate, p, is 1 per cent and that a firm has borrowed £1000. If there is no inflation, the firm's interest payments are £10. Now suppose that inflation (p) rises to 10 per cent and that the nominal interest rate (r) is given by the formulae $(1+r) = (1+p)(1+p)$. Then r rises to 11.1 per cent and total interest payments to £111. Hence, at a time when revenue has risen by only 10 per cent interest payments rise elevenfold, and this creates cashflow problems for the firm.

None of this would matter if the firm could simply borrow an extra £100, leaving it to find only £11, a rise of 10 per cent, equal to its own increase in revenue. In an inefficient capital market banks are not likely to be so accommodating and companies face an increased probability of failure.

Wadhwani (op. cit.) does not introduce inflation directly into his regressions, but nominal and real interest rates. The former would seem to have had a strong influence on the incidence of liquidations, but the statistical significance of real interest rates would seem to have been affected by which other variables were included in the model, which does not suggest a strong relationship.

Simmons (1989) developed Wadhwani's model further but his empirical results are not overwhelming in the support they provide for the effect of inflation on business failure. When the incidence of personal bankruptcies which, by implication, Simmons believed to be synonymous with business failure were considered separately in four sectors, inflation either did not appear to have made any difference or to have been related negatively, i.e. the incidence of bankruptcy fell with increases in the price level.

Similarly, when various measures of interest rates were introduced they usually appeared to have had the opposite impact on bankruptcies from what would be expected from Wadhwani's model. When considering creditors' voluntary and compulsory liquidations separately Hudson (1987) found the former to have had either no relationship or a negative one with interest rates, but the relationship with compulsory liquidation appeared to be strongly negative.

Some insight into the possible reason for the apparently counter-intuitive relationship between interest rates and business failure are supplied by Stiglitz and Weiss (1981). They centre on the type of companies that would be likely to be least deterred by high interest rates, which would certainly include those in distress.

Both Wadhwani (op. cit.) and Simmons (op. cit.) introduce measures of input prices and levels of demand into their models. The relationships with business failure are usually as would be expected, positive and negative, respectively. It is reassuring for intuition to be confirmed – that factors exogenous to firms will affect their chances of survival, that it is not just a matter of the efficiency of their management. However, as the results of Wadhwani (op. cit.) and Simmons (1989) are not standardised in any way it is not possible to compare the coefficients in their models, and hence infer the relative importance of the variables. As this was not the intention of either author this certainly should not be interpreted as a criticism. Resolution of this important question must, however, await the results of future research.

CONCLUDING REMARKS

To answer the question that constitutes the title of this chapter, we do not really know very much. Experts who base their opinions on experience of dealing with small firms are divided in the conclusions that they draw. Irrespective of whether prediction models are effective at meeting their purposes they do not provide many insights into the causes of failure. Empirical studies of aggregate failure would not, on the whole, suggest rises in interest rates to be positively associated with the number of failures, in fact, possibly the reverse, but otherwise only reveal that increases in costs or falls in demand can lead to business failure.

The next two chapters may shed a little more light on this area.

4

WHAT OFFICIAL RECEIVER'S REPORTS REVEAL ABOUT FAILURE[1]

This chapter will make a modest attempt to add to our knowledge of why small firms fail by drawing on the information contained in the reports of the Official Receiver. These reports must be made on all cases of 'compulsory liquidation' where liquidation is forced by a court order. In order to pre-empt the unpleasantness that this situation might imply, the owners may agree to enter into a 'creditors' voluntary liquidation'. The difficulty of distinguishing between both types of liquidation is recognized by Hudson (1987) who argued, 'It is largely a matter of chance in which category an insolvent firm will fall'. If this is the case one can be fairly sanguine that facts revealed about compulsory liquidations would be equally valid for creditors' voluntary liquidations, which, in 1983, together represented 72 per cent of the notifications to start liquidation proceedings.

The balance consists of 'members' voluntary' liquidations, in which the initiative comes from the owners of companies, who undertake to meet their companies' debts within the following twelve months. Those failing to honour this understanding would then reappear in one of the other categories. It is not possible to identify how far the characteristics of firms that succeed in meeting their debts differ from those liquidated compulsorily or through creditors' voluntary liquidations .

Liquidations arise where cessation of trading is accompanied by the disposal of assets. Most corporate closures, three-quarters in 1983, are struck off from the register of companies because they have failed to file their annual returns and/or failed to pay the modest annual registration fee. It is likely that many of these companies never, in fact, enjoyed a corporate life of any significance and they should not, therefore, be described as having failed (Storey, Keasey, Watson and Wynarczk, 1987). There is no way of knowing the extent that the data

30

on companies experiencing compulsory liquidation would be pertinent to those that traded for some period, but which were allowed to
die quietly by their owners without any formal liquidation proceedings.

This chapter is based on a study of 1064 reports disaggregated into
278, 385 and 401 for 1973, 1978 and 1983, respectively, and 300, 243,
258 and 263 for London, the Midlands, North West and South West,
respectively. All values have been inflated to their equivalent at 1988
prices. It was originally intended to draw a sample of 300 cases for
each region from each year but, outside the London area, pre-1983
records have not always been fully maintained. The 1985 *Companies Act*
considerably reduced the information contained in Official Receiver's
reports, rendering impossible comparisons with more recent years.

What is surprising is the lack of common information, even pre-
1985. Within the sample of reports the only information that is
common to all is the year of insolvency and the number of years that
the company traded. Fortunately there was sufficient on the amount
of unsecured loans at insolvency, and the reasons for failure as perceived by owners and by the Official Receiver, to be able to draw
statistically valid results.

SIZE AND INSOLVENCY

For the 738 cases that supplied such information (N=738) the mean
value of their assets at the point of insolvency was £54,767, the median
£6,319 and the standard deviation £184,127. Only seven had assets of above
£1,000,000 and the maximum was £2,870,000. Given the difficulties in
valuing assets and the likelihood that owners of failing firms might be
expected to dispose of whatever assets they can before the instigation
of formal insolvency proceedings, turnover in previous years would be
a more reliable measure of the size of failed firms, but this is not usually
supplied at all or, if so, only idiosyncratically within the five years
prior to insolvency. The most commonly cited year (N=307) is the
third before insolvency. One might have expected that only the largest
firms would supply such information, but the mean value of revenue
was, nevertheless only £650,000, the median £205,000 and the standard deviation £1,223,000. The maximum was just over £11,000,000.

A more comprehensive (N=1050) but indirect measure of size is
the amount owed that is not secured against assets. The mean was
£414,000, the median £47,000 and the standard deviation £3,271,000,
reflecting the outer maximum of £60 million, though in only twenty-
nine cases was more than a million pounds owed. Clearly, only small

firms would fail for such generally small amounts. As would be predicted by most theory and has been confirmed by all previous studies, failure is almost entirely confined to the small-firm sector.

It is possible that, over time, changes have taken place in the distribution by size of failures, perhaps because a change has occurred in the critical growth path suggested by Jovanovic (1982) and discussed in Chapter 2, perhaps the environment surrounding the small-firm sector may have become more or less benevolent with consequent changes in the distribution of failures across size bands. When the amount owed is banded into <£50,000, £50,000–£99,999 and £100,000+ there is no statistically significant[2] difference over time in the distribution of failures by size. In real terms, the distribution of the levels of unsecured debt faced by insolvent companies, and, therefore, by implication, the distribution of their size, did not change between 1973 and 1983.

Given that the level of output that must be achieved in order to obtain lowest costs will vary across sectors, one would expect this to be reflected between sectors in the average size of insolvencies. Maintaining the same bands as above, and the surrogate for size of amount owed, this would appear to be precisely the case. Table 4.1 shows how the amounts of unsecured loans vary across sectors. A '+' indicates at least five more companies in this cell than would be expected given the breakdown within the sample as a whole, '–' at least five less.[3] On this definition there is a 'bias' towards failing among small general merchandisers and those firms operating in construction. Property/land developers and manufacturers are likely to be in the biggest size band, whereas retailers display a bias towards the middle band.

As will be shown below, there are regional differences in the numbers of insolvencies occurring across industrial sectors and this is a possible explanation for the marked difference between regions in

Table 4.1 Size (unsecured loans) by sector

£	Property developers	General merchandisers	Retailers	Construction	Manufacturers
<50,000		+		+	–
50,000– 99,999		–	+	+	
100,000+	+			–	+

No bias in exporters/importers, catering, professional services and other.

the amount owed. In London and the south–west the bias is towards firms being rendered insolvent for the sake of relatively small amounts, whereas in the Midlands and the north–west the reverse is true (Table 4.2).

Table 4.2 Size (unsecured loans) by region

	£		
	<50,000	50,000–99,999	100,000+
London	+	−	−
Midlands	−		+
North-west	−		+
South-west	+		−

NUMBER OF YEARS TRADED (N=1064)

The mean lifespan of the insolvencies was 6.79 years, the median, four years and the standard deviation was 8.2 years. One hundred and eighty-six had traded for 10 or more years, 30 for 30 years or more and the longest for 66 years. The mean should be compared with the 2.3 years which Ganguly (1985) derived from VAT registrations. Such registrations, Ganguly readily concedes, provide only an approximate and partial indication of corporate life and, it would seem, an underestimate of the length of average lifespan.

Although Jovanovic (op. cit.) does not specify any sort of timeframe, a period of almost seven years would seem somewhat longer than might be expected before the full impact of a failure to achieve a critical growth path was experienced. It would, however, represent a credible period in which are revealed the inadequacies of the management team in dealing with problems which were not anticipated at the inception of the company. As argued in Chapter 2, the portfolio of management skills within a small firm, which in the smallest may be concentrated in a single owner, may be adequate for founding a company, for predicting and successfully managing the problems with which it is initially confronted, but may be inadequate for coping with problems that arise at later stages of its life. It would appear that, in so far as this represents the process leading to failure, unexpected (or at least unmanageable) shocks on average assault small firms within approximately the first seven years of their life, though, given the lag that occurs between experiencing a shock and succumbing to its effects, it is not possible to identify exactly when.

The severity of external shocks, or degree of turbulence in the environment which surrounds small firms could easily vary over time, with consequent changes in their average lifespan. Some improvement in the conditions facing small firms between 1973–1983 is indeed suggested by the increase in the average lifespan of insolvencies suggested by Table 4.3.

Table 4.3 Number of years traded by year of insolvency

Years	1973	1978	1983
<5	+	+	−
5–9	−	+	
10+	−	−	+

It is quite clear that the average lifespan of insolvencies varies between sectors (Table 4.4). Exporters/importers, retailers and general merchandisers display a bias towards failure within their first five years of life; companies operating in the professions and construction industry are susceptible to failure in their first ten years and property/land developers and manufacturers contain a greater number of firms surviving for more than ten years than would be expected from the performance of the total sample.

Several explanations are possible for these differences. It may be more difficult in some sectors than in others to achieve the critical growth path suggested by Jovanovic (op. cit.) perhaps because of differences in moving along the learning curve that his theory implies. Alternatively, the difficulties confronted in jumping between stages in a company's development, especially between start-up and sustained growth, may vary between sectors. Lastly, during the period considered, the effects of external shocks, or of turbulence, may have been more severe in some sectors than in others.

One rather surprising discovery is that the distribution of lifespans did not vary between regions.[4] The uneven distribution of sectors across regions might have led to the opposite expectation. One possibility is that differences between the economic climates of regions in their degree of benevolence towards small firms may, coincidentally, counter-balance differences between sectors, but this is purely a matter of conjecture.

Table 4.4 Number of years traded by sector

Years	Exporters/Importers	Retailers	Property sector	General merchandisers	Manufacturing	Professional services	Construction	Other
<5	+	+	-	+	-			-
5–9		-				+	+	+
10+		-	+	-	+	-	-	

SECTORS IN WHICH FAILURE TOOK PLACE

Two features are striking. First, over two-fifths of the insolvencies were in construction. This sector is undoubtedly particularly vulnerable to failure. The type of firms that fail in construction will be discussed in the next chapter. Second, after construction there is no single sector displaying a similar obvious vulnerability. The percentages of the total sample represented by the next seven sectors in which involuntary insolvency was most common were:

- Property/land developers 6.9.
- General merchants 6.0.
- Manufacturing 5.5.
- Garage proprietors 4.5.
- Haulage contractors 3.9.
- Importers/exporters 3.9.
- Electrical engineers 3.8.

Not surprisingly, over time changes have occurred in the distribution of the relative numbers of failures across sectors. Alternative reasons could be:

- Changes in the relative number of companies operating in each sector, resulting in changes in the relative numbers of insolvencies even if the incidence of failures remains the same.
- Sectors displaying uneven reactions to movements in the economic climate.
- Alteration in conditions facing individual markets. Some of these alterations could prove beneficial to small-firm survival, others harmful. Some clues as to the relative importance of these factors will be supplied in the next section.

Whatever the reason, considering the differences between the number of insolvencies experienced and the number to be expected given the proportion of each sector in the total sample (Table 4.5):

- 1978 proved a bad[5] year for property developers and 1983 good.
- 1973 was good for general merchandisers but 1983 was bad.
- 1978 was good for manufacturing but 1983 was bad.
- Companies offering professional services did badly in 1973 but well in 1978.
- Construction did badly in 1978 but well in 1983.

There are marked regional differences in the distribution of failures

Table 4.5 Year of insolvency by sector

	Retailers	Property developers	General merchandisers	Manufacturing	Professional services	Construction	Other
1973	+		−		+		+
1978		+		−	−	+	−
1983		−	+	+		−	

Note: Catering showed no bias

Table 4.6 Sector by region

	Exporters Importers	Retailers	Property developers	Catering	Manufacturing	Construction	Other
London			+		–		–
Midlands	+	–	–	–	+		+
North-west	–		–		+	–	+
South-west				+	–	+	

General merchandisers and professional services displayed no bias

Table 4.7   Reasons for failure – owners' perceptions

Operational Management	
Under–capitalization	235
Poor management of debt	111
Inaccurate costing and estimating	34
Poor management accounting	23
Poor supervision of staff	8
Overstocking	7
Late delivery of materials	6
Loss of experienced personnel	3
Skill shortages of staff	7
	434
Strategic	
Lack of demand for products	66
Funding associated companies	44
Reliance on a few customers	28
Competitor behaviour	27
Reliance on a few suppliers	11
New entrants into market	1
	177
Environmental	
High interest rates	37
Fire	14
Theft	10
Exchange rates	2
Flood	1
	64
Personal	
Disagreement with partners	26
Ill-health	21
Excessive remuneration	15
	62
Technological	
Inferior product	25
No previous knowledge or experience	17
Use of inferior materials	7
Inferior plant	4
	53
Marketing	
Poor forecasting	30
Under pricing	10
Adverse publicity	4
Over pricing	2
	46
Rises in	
Overhead costs	11
Operating costs	4
Fixed costs	2
Labour costs	2
Material costs	2
	21

Owners perceptions of failure (N=857)

across sectors (Table 4.6). This presumably reflects differences in the distribution of activities throughout the country but there could also be variations between regions in the conditions facing particular sectors. London clearly displays a bias towards failure among property developers and against failure among manufacturers.

In the Midlands insolvencies were higher than would be expected among exporters/importers and manufacturers, but lower among retailers, property developers and caterers. In the north-west the bias was towards failure among manufacturers and away from failure among property developers and construction companies, whereas in the south-west caterers and construction companies suffered particularly badly but exporters/importers and manufacturers enjoyed fewer failures than would be expected.

Perhaps the most interesting information contained in the Official Receivers' reports is the opinions of owners on why their companies had failed (Table 4.7). One would not expect a great deal of objectivity nor probably expertise in their interpretation of the circumstances surrounding their companies' failure, but this does not mean that their perceptions are without foundation. They are especially of value when comparisons are made between the various groups making up the total sample. Whatever the bias in the opinions of owners, there are no compelling reasons for its degree to vary over time or between types of companies.

What is immediately quite surprising about the reasons provided by owners (see Table 4.7) is how little blame is assigned to factors which might be described as beyond their control, such as interest and exchange rates, other sources of rising costs, or even ill-health or disagreement with partners.

About half of the owners, whose opinions were presented on the reports, identified as crucial problems centring on their operational management. Of these problems, under-capitalization was by far the most important. This can be translated into an inability to carry on business effectively because of insufficient funds. There could be any of four quite distinct reasons for this:

1   Poor estimation of the capital needs of a company, either at its inception or at some later stage.
2   Correct estimation, but shortcomings in their negotiating skills meant that owners could not convince their banks of the soundness of their case.

3 Their bank correctly identified that the company was a probable loser, and sensibly refrained from making a major commitment.
4 Their bank did not provide sufficient funds for what would have been a viable business. It incorrectly identified the company as a probable loser.

Of these, the third is the least plausible. If a company, whether at its start-up, or when up and running, appears to be a loser its bank is unlikely to make any level of investment; it is not the habit of bank managers to make small bets at long odds on the chance that they might pay off. Yet there is no evidence that failed companies were completely starved of bank support and have had to rely on whatever capital they could generate from personal resources or from friends and relatives.

Turning to the other explanations, it is certainly no mean feat to make an accurate prediction of capital requirements. Whereas expenditure on major items of equipment is unlikely to come as a complete surprise it is much more difficult to know with certainty what the cashflow position will be at some point in the future, particularly given the vulnerability of small firms to late payment by customers. Changes in demand and cost conditions are even more difficult to forecast. This would be the case for a large company with all the skills of a planning department at its disposal; it is even more so for small firms, in which the sum total of forecasting techniques will probably be little more sophisticated than intuition.

One of the benefits, however, of an effective banking system is that temporary excess of cost over revenue should not matter. Certainly, the management of cashflow should present no problems as long as there are not serious doubts about the likelihood of receiving late payments. Banks would readily lend on the basis of outstanding invoices. Even adverse shocks to revenue and cost flows should not matter too much if the chances are that they will be eventually balanced by shocks that are beneficial.

The information in the Official Receiver reports is insufficient to judge whether the failed companies were victims of an unreasonableness from banks to help them survive temporary deficits in their cashflow or victims of a conservativeness from banks in their evaluation of whether bad luck would be followed by good or, on the other hand, whether banks were simply exercising sound commercial judgement. What may be of some significance, however, is the low emphasis that owners have put on factors that would represent shocks to their income streams.

This might suggest lack of capital to be a problem in its own right rather than as the result of some traumatic event. Moreover, after 'under-capitalization' the most frequently cited reason for failure was 'poor management of debt' which, if there were an effective banking system, would only represent a problem to the extent that credit were extended to customers that ultimately defaulted on payment.

Turning to the other reasons provided by owners for their companies' failure, strategic issues come a distant second behind operational management, with competitor behaviour and entrance into their markets by new customers being cited very infrequently. This is somewhat surprising given the high weighting to such issues within the management literature. Technological and marketing problems are also blamed far less than would be expected but whether this is evidence of their actual unimportance, or to the ignorance of its importance amongst owners, must remain an open question.

The question mark hanging over the reliability of owners' perceptions has less significance when comparisons are made between sub-groups within the sample as long as the direction and degree of any unreliability remains approximately the same. Owners whose firms failed within their first five years were more likely to blame operational, technological and marketing reasons, and less strategic (Table 4.8). In other words they were not initially taken by surprise by factors, such as lack of demand and entrance of new competitors, but they did face problems in the day-to-day running of their companies, especially from lack of capital, problems centring on the quality of their products and those associated with the launch of their products. However, as their companies increased in age they were more likely to be confronted by strategic problems which they would regard as sufficiently serious to cause their failure. Owners of older companies were also more likely to lay the blame on environmental factors, especially high interest rates.

If these differences within the life of companies have any validity it would seem that owners who had proved able to launch their companies successfully had not possessed the capability to survive shocks to their revenue streams, such as fall in demand or entrance of new competitors, or shocks to their cost streams, such as increase in interest rates.

Quite marked differences are revealed when the sample is disaggregated by size (Table 4.9). The owners of the smallest companies, those

Table 4.8 Directors' reasons and number of years traded

Years	Operational management	Strategic	Technological	Marketing sales	Personal	Environmental
<5	+	−	+	+	−	−
5–9	−	+		+		
10+	−	+	−			+

There was no bias by years traded towards costs of production problems

Table 4.9 Size (unsecured loans) and Directors' reasons

£	Operational management	Strategic	Costs of production	Technological	Personal	Environmental
<50,000	−	−			+	−
50,000–99,999			+	+		
100,000+	+	+	−	−	−	+

with unsecured loans of less then £50,000, were more likely to blame personal factors, such as disagreement with partners or ill-health, and technological factors, usually centring on the quality of their products, and less likely operational, strategic and environmental ones. Vice versa, owners of firms owing above £100,000.

There was no bias of Marketing/Sales problems to particular size ranges. Not surprisingly, it is the smallest companies which are the most vulnerable to direct disruptions to their portfolio of management skills – which may, of course, be concentrated in a single person – and it would appear that their owners demonstrate the most willingness to acknowledge the inadequacy of their products.

When the reasons are considered for failure in each of the three years encompassed by the study it is clear that changes have occurred (Table 4.10). The oil price increases of the early 1970s appear to have been reflected in operational problems rather than those factors here classified as environmental. The early 1970s were also characterized by a higher incidence of personal problems, though there is no way of knowing whether these were associated with the traumas of the increase in oil prices. The 1980s, on the other hand, would appear to be characterized by both an increase in the severity of shocks, strategic and environmental, and by an improvement in the operational management of companies.

Table 4.10 Directors' reasons and year of insolvency

	1973	1978	1983
Operational	+	+	−
Strategic		−	+
Personal	+		
Environmental	−		+

There was no bias by year of insolvency towards cost of production, technological or marketing/sales reasons

There are significant differences between regions in the distribution of reasons given by owners for their companies' failure (Table 4.11). In London, strategic and technological reasons figured much higher than would be expected and operational management lower. In the Midlands, operational management was more important and

Table 4.11 Directors' reasons by region

	Operational management	Strategic	Technological	Marketing/ Sales	Personal
London	–	+	+		
Midlands	+			–	–
North-west	–			+	+
South-west	+			–	

There was no bias of cost or environmental reasons towards particular regions

marketing and personal less. In the north-west marketing and personal problems were more than would be expected from the sample as a whole, and operational management less, wheras in the south-west, operational management was higher than expected.

These differences could reflect variations between regions on a host of dimensions, the most obvious being the distribution of sectors. Unfortunately, for purely technical reasons[6] it is not possible to state with certainty whether there are statistically significant differences in the distribution of reasons between sectors. For this reason the results are not shown in tabular form. Nevertheless, there would appear to be some marked differences, even if these cannot be confirmed rigorously. Retailers cited problems in marketing more than would be expected; property developers cited environmental problems more and operational less; caterers operational less; professionals marketing more; and construction companies operational problems more, but strategic, marketing and environmental less.

THE PERCEPTIONS OF THE OFFICIAL RECEIVER

Almost invariably, the reports from the Official Receiver contain their opinions as to why failure occurred. Their analysis will obviously reflect their breadth of experience and should be devoid of any bias towards portraying events in the best possible light for owners. They may, however, contain a different sort of bias. Official Receivers are usually accountancy trained. Their analysis may well reflect this background, as would a training in any other management discipline. Hence, it may be argued, it is not surprising that in almost half the cases failure was blamed on under-capitalization, because of the emphasis within accountancy on the need for an adequate provision of capital. Accountants are less likely to look beyond financial statements for the reasons for shortages in capital.

Nevertheless, even with this handful of salt, the confirmation of the importance of under-capitalization cannot be ignored. Even if there were an inherent bias within the interpretation of events provided by the Official Receiver variations continue between sub-groups within the sample. These are broadly consistent with those displayed by the opinions of owners.

The Official Receiver concurs with owners on the importance of operational reasons in causing failure among start-ups while strategic reasons figure much more prominently among companies over ten years of age. Other differences were not so marked as occurred within the opinions of owners. When the sample is broken down by size, the Official Receivers agree as to the vulnerability of the smallest companies to the personal problems hitting their owners but do not share their opinions as to the importance of technological problems. The Official Receivers agree as to the relatively higher incidence of strategic and environmental reasons among larger firms but considered operational management as posing particular problems for companies in the middle of the size bands, i.e. those with unsecured loans of £50,000–£100,000. This area would appear as slightly less important for companies either side of this range. Otherwise, there were not any particularly marked differences between the size bands.

Significant differences do, however, occur between opinions of owners and Official Receivers as to the distribution of reasons over time. Although they are consistent on the decreasing importance between 1973–1983 of personal problems in causing failure, the Official Receiver regarded operational problems as increasing over time, and strategic as decreasing – quite the reverse from what would be concluded from the opinions of owners. This is the only area in which significant disagreement occurs between the two sets of opinions, except in so far as the Official Receivers' perceptions of the reasons for failure do not differ so markedly between sectors and hardly at all between regions.

CONCLUDING REMARKS

The Official Receiver's reports contain objective data from which some useful conclusions can be drawn, specifically:

- The value of unsecured loans that are outstanding to firms involuntarily liquidated varied across sectors and regions.
- The number of years traded varied over time and across sectors.
- The incidence of failure within sectors varied over time and across regions.

Perhaps rather more interesting, however, are the opinions of the owners of insolvent firms on why failure took place. Although this may be analogous to asking patients why they are ill (or, more accurately, have died!) such information is not without value especially in the light of differences in responses over time and between sub-groups and of the extent the opinions of owners concurs with that exhibited by the Official Receivers themselves. Owners most commonly lay the blame for their failure on operational reasons, in particular on under-capitalization, and the Official Receivers usually agree with this assessment. Such problems would appear to be more important in the early stages of a company's life. After these the emphasis shifts to the strategic, personal and environmental. It is not just a matter of size, however. If amount owed is used as surrogate for size it was the owners of the biggest firms that were more likely to identify operational, strategic and environmental problems for their failure, whereas the smallest identified technological and personal. There was also some evidence of operational, possibly personal, problems assuming less importance between periods and strategic and environmental more.

5

WHICH FIRMS FAIL: THE CASE OF CONSTRUCTION[1]

Chapter 3 contained the observations that the failure prediction literature reveals little about why any firms fail, including small firms, and that the writers who have directly addressed this question often do not employ very sound methodology, though there are some notable exceptions. The major weakness is that writers, at best, draw their conclusions about why firms fail from a sample of firms that have failed, without any comparison with a control group of survivors and, at worst, simply draw on their personal experience. Concentrating on a sample of failures may identify their weaknesses but these weaknesses may be common to all small firms, and not the causes of the companies failing.

This chapter will discuss the results of trying to establish the factors distinguishing survivors from failures in the UK construction sector. It is highly desirable to draw all of the companies from the same sector because of the likelihood that the incidence of failure will be affected by both the height of barriers to entry and by market-specific conditions. Certainly, it is hard to envisage employing a common questionnaire across sectors when the precise form taken by each of the branches of management can so easily differ. That does not imply, however, that research may not show that regardless of sector efficiency in one specific branch is usually more important in ensuring survival than efficiency in another, or that within each of the management disciplines there are not particular approaches which are usually important. A niche strategy, for instance, could be shown to be generally associated with survival, even though the form that this might take will vary across sectors.

Construction was chosen because after retailing it suffers the highest absolute number of VAT deregistrations (Daly, 1991) and whilst its ratio of deregistrations to the total stock of its registered companies is marginally below that across all sectors (48 per cent against 50 per cent) the proportion that its involuntary insolvencies form of the total number of involuntary insolvencies is significantly higher than the proportion that its VAT deregistrations form of total deregistrations. Chapter 4 showed that in 1983 involuntary insolvencies in construction represented 42 per cent of the total in the four regions considered; this should be compared with 13 per cent of the total number of VAT deregistrations for that year (Daly, *op. cit.*).

It is not surprising that this sector should suffer such a high volume of VAT deregistrations or be so vulnerable to involuntary insolvency. Testimony to its low barriers to entry is provided by its high stock of VAT-registered companies, again second only to retailing. Yet it has suffered a long term contraction in output, the problems from which are exacerbated by the highly uncertain environment in which it operates. Not only are its fortunes particularly sensitive to the vagaries of government policy and the state of the economy, but construction companies are denied some of the usual avenues for compensating for fluctuating demand. Unsold buildings, for instance, do not represent a very commercially attractive form of stock-building, and aggressive proactive marketing is not a common feature of the sector, especially those segments of the market in which tradition dictates competitive tendering.

The remainder of this chapter will consist of a description of methodology, explanation of the choice of variables and discussion of results.

METHODOLOGY

Data was collected through personal interviews,[2] carried out between December 1989 and February 1990, inclusive, with the owners of twenty-eight firms that had ceased to trade during the previous five years and a control group of thirty firms that had survived. Because the likelihood of a firm failing decreases with its age, the two samples were matched by start-up date. All firms operated in the north-west of England. Clearly, whilst it may be desirable to hold constant inter-regional differences in factors associated with survival in order to produce a clearer picture with respect to a particular region, if such differences are important, the validity of generalizing from the results is correspondingly reduced.

The firms were all small, employing a workforce of less than 100, usually much less. The owners of the failed firms were identified through the Dun and Bradstreet database; those of the survivors from a wide range of sources.[3] This was necessitated by the size of the sample which initially needed to be surveyed in order to generate an adequately sized control group of companies with matching start-up dates. This did not produce any obvious bias. On the other hand, data on both failures and survivors could, self-evidently, only be collected from owners who were willing to be interviewed. This must, unavoidably, produce a bias away from owners who, for whatever reason, might not wish to discuss the running of their business. This study also completely ignores the 'black' economy which, in UK construction, is not trivial.

The data was analysed in two ways. First, through forward stepwise logit regression. Because of the large number of variables on which data had been collected, these were divided into halves (odd- and even-numbered variables, respectively) and the computer package scanned the data for the variable in each half with the strongest statistical association with whether or not a company survived, then the next most important, and so on. For instance, to take a hypothetical example, if all of the owners of surviving companies possessed a degree, and all of the owners of failures did not, the importance of this variable would be identified early on in the process. If, on the other hand, it was merely the case that more owners of surviving companies possessed degrees than owners of failures the variable might not figure at all in the results.

The most important from each half of the variables were then pooled and the process repeated. It is a well-known weakness of stepwise processes that they can produce results which are largely a matter of chance and are not replicable on other samples. As a test for consistency, therefore, the process was repeated on two sub-samples of forty-eight companies, randomly chosen.

The second way that the data was analysed was to examine whether there were any principal components within the variables. This is a way of grouping together those factors which, within a sample, are usually found together. If, for instance, owners with degrees commonly are prompt in paying their bills, price their work strategically, adopt a computerized information system and have a high proportion of skilled workers on their payroll, these variables might be grouped together as a principal component. If such a combination were more likely to occur among the survivors or the failures the principal component could be employed, as if it were a single variable, in a logit regression.

As will be discussed later, it was not possible to identify any principal components that were meaningful or helpful and the methodology was limited to stepwise regression. It must be emphasized that the absence of a variable from the results does not indicate that it does not make any difference as to whether a company survives, only that it is not one of the set of variables that collectively would appear to make most difference. Naturally, as with all statistically based approaches, a strong relationship does not necessarily indicate causality. Although the assumption behind this study was precisely that the presence of a factor among survivors, and absence among failures, would suggest that it made a difference to the probability of survival, it would not be difficult with ingenuity to argue for a different reason for the relationship.

Choice of variables

As was suggested in Chapter 3, a case has been made for the chances of survival being affected by a range of factors and the list grows much longer when the boundaries of a review are extended to encompass the literature on the influences on performance in general (see Chapters 6–10). Although it does not follow that the factors associated with the growth or profitability of a small firm will necessarily be the same as those determining whether it survives, it would be surprising if they were not related.

Personal

Whereas it would undoubtedly have proved very helpful to have included if it were possible owner personality as a variable it was decided to focus attention on factors on which data could be collected straightforwardly through interview rather than through in-depth techniques, such as psychometric testing, on which later chapters will express strong scepticism. Those tests that were included are given some theoretical underpinning by Jovanovic's (1982) learning curve model of survival which predicts a positive correlation between the volume of human capital embodied in senior management and the probability of survival.

Human capital is a broad term encompassing all the capabilities of a person. Questions were put, therefore, on a wide range of factors which might increase these capabilities:

- The age of owners when they started the business. This might be expected to be positively related to the probability of their companies' survival, though Bates (1990) found the optimum age for a sample of American entrepreneurs to be 45–55. To establish which of these hypotheses would be the more valid with respect to UK construction the model was specified as both a straight-line and U-shaped relationship.
- Their education levels, including whether they had attended any sort of management training course.
- Whether owners had had previous experience of management, had previously managed a construction business, had owned one, and whether this had failed, though one could argue either way on whether this would be likely to reduce the likelihood of failure being repeated.
- The number of owners who worked directly in the business. This follows Argenti's (1976) argument that the greater the number of senior decision-makers, the less likely failure.
- The skill levels of the workforce. The volume of human capital embodied in a business will include the capabilities of its employees as well as that of its owners. Questions covered the proportions with various qualifications and the number and experience of foremen. Questions also covered the related issue of the proportion of employees who had received their training within the company, on the assumption that a commitment to staff development would probably reduce the probability of failure.

Outside assistance

One way to supplement the volume of human capital at the disposal of a company is to employ or consult experts on an *ad hoc* basis and there is empirical evidence to demonstrate the benefits from doing so (Robinson, 1982).

Data was collected on whether outsiders were employed to carry out bookkeeping, the preparation of internal and published accounts and the provision of information for the Inland Revenue or to provide advice on legal matters. Further questions covered the extent that advice was taken before starting the company and whether this was provided by an accountant, lawyer or a bank.

Motivation

As will be discussed in Chapter 6, the motivation of owners for starting or assuming control of their business may play some part in determining their success. Even though hindsight may colour their memories, it would seem too important an area to omit from the study.

The alternatives presented to interviewees were that they started or assumed control:

- To earn a higher income than from previous employment or business.
- To become their own boss.
- Through lack of choice (though this included the occasional business handed down from fathers).
- Through redundancy.
- As a sideline or hobby.

It was assumed that owners motivated by the first two would be more likely to survive than if motivated by the more half-hearted other three.

Strategic management

In the construction sector subcontracting plays an important role. In a seminal paper Coase (1937) considers the circumstances under which firms will employ people on a permanent basis and those under which they will rely on contracts to carry out specific items of work. The latter is far more common in construction than in other major sectors. Subcontracting to other firms provides flexibility in the size of the labour force and hence in the volume of overheads, clearly an advantage in such a volatile sector.

It represents an appropriate strategy to the extent that the performance of the subcontractors will not be lower than if they had been full-time employees. It is possible to divide up a project into self-contained, precisely defined assignments – plumbing, brickwork, tarmacadaming or whatever – but performance may be affected if the threat of legal action proves a stronger or weaker motivator than the loyalty, and greater flexibility as to the work undertaken, resulting from permanent employment.

Construction firms must decide not only how much work they will subcontract but the extent they will rely on work subcontracted to them. A commitment to subcontracted work will represent the appropriate route for companies lacking the skills to win contracts from the ultimate customer or capital to build in anticipation of a sale, and it will probably provide a more steady income. The scope for added value, on the other hand, will reduce with the position down the chain from the final customer.

Construction companies, in common with those in most other sectors, face a trade-off between the advantages from specialization and those from offering a range of services. The former will improve the capability to carry out a specific activity but can prove vulnerable to a decline in demand. In order to establish whether flexibility represents a key to survival, further questions were put on whether the range of services offered had broadened over time.

The other area covered was the distribution of turnover between the public and private sectors, the broadest segments within the market.

The variable which, with the benefit of hindsight, would have been included in the study was the number of activities carried out. Reid (1993) found in his sample of small Scottish companies that survival was positively correlated with the number of product groups supplied.

Marketing

The interviews encompassed three areas of marketing. The first was the means by which business was secured, the alternatives being word of mouth, proactive selling and, at the other end of the spectrum, simply being listed in British Telecom's *Yellow Pages*. The second area was the extent of pre-launch marketing. Interviewees were asked the number of their potential customers who they could identify before their companies were founded and the proportion of the first year turnover that came from these customers. The assumption was that companies were more likely to survive the highly vulnerable start-up period the less their uncertainty about the initial level of demand they would face.

Pricing was the third area of marketing included in the study. Though it represents the linchpin of micro-economics the techniques that should be employed are given scant attention within most marketing textbooks. This study worked on the premise that pricing should be strategic, influenced by the behaviour of competition and intended to secure repeat business. Owners would be less likely to succeed if their pricing strategy was limited to securing a pre-determined profit on full costs. Costing is not, however, an easy exercise in construction and questions were also included on who actually carried this out: an internally or externally employed quantity surveyor, the owner, or a member of staff not qualified as a quantity surveyor. The expectation was that costing should be carried out by an expert, though with the recognition that the personal involvement of the owner in such a crucial task might prove preferable even if he is not formally qualified.

As a further measure of marketing orientation the proportion of revenue devoted to marketing was established.

Financial management

This was covered in some depth in the study. One set of questions was intended to establish the degree of sophistication of the financial information that was available to owners; whether they maintained separate personal and business accounts, regarded in the study as the absolute minimum level of prudency in the management of finances; and whether their financial information was derived from:

- A cashbook, bank statement or bills/invoices.
- Double entry bookkeeping, including sales and purchase ledgers.
- Monthly or quarterly management accounts.
- Fully computerized accounts.

The expectation was that the use of sophisticated information would be associated with a greater probability of survival.

The availability of information is not, of course, any indication of the uses to which it is put. Interviewees were asked, therefore, to weight the importance of the following alternatives by allocating a hundred points between them.

Financial information was produced to:

- Satisfy the Inland Revenue.
- Assist in negotiations with trade creditors.
- Facilitate the raising of finance.
- Confirm the accuracy of other records.
- Monitor the performance of the company.

The expectation was that owners who collected financial information primarily to help in the running of their businesses would be more likely to survive than those limiting its use to assisting in their nego-tiations with external parties.

Another dimension of financial information is the frequency with which it is collected, *ceteris paribus* the more frequently the better, and the identity of the person responsible for its collection. As with other important areas, such as costing, it may be preferable for the collation of financial information to be carried out by experts, in this case an accountant, or by the owner himself, which may reflect the importance he attaches to this task; given the skill needed for such collation, the former probably represents the safer route. Certainly, it would seem preferable that either an accountant or the owner carried out the task rather than this being delegated to an employee not trained in accountancy.

Of possible equal importance to the quality of financial informa-tion in the running of a small firm is the skill with which its cashflow is managed. The timing of payments and receipts, especially in the absence of a sympathetic bank manager, may be as crucial to survival as their volume. Hence, questions were put on the percentages of purchases made on credit, and of sales provided on credit, and on the time taken on average for interviewees to pay bills and before they would expect their own invoices to be paid.

A further aspect of the management of cashflow is the treatment of surpluses. Firms would seem more likely to survive the greater the proportion of surpluses ploughed back into the running of the busi-ness, rather than taken as remuneration by owners. As well as a direct question on this, a related question covered whether owners were on a fixed salary. Providing it is set at a reasonable level, a fixed salary can ease the management of cashflow by rendering it a little less unpre-dictable and by helping owners to resist the temptation to cream off profits as personal income. On the other hand, owners might prove inflexible in their expectations about what is a reasonable income when falling returns necessitate a cut.

Relations with the bank

The adequacy of the banking sector in meeting the needs of small firms is subject to fierce debate.[4] Obviously, the survey, on which this study is based, could not be expected to make any serious inroads into such a complex issue, but it might be illuminating to establish whether owners' perceptions of the attitude of banks was an important dis-criminator between survivors and failures even though it would not provide any indication as to whether these attitudes were well-founded. If the owners of failures generally perceived their banks as unhelpful, and owners of survivors perceived theirs as helpful, this does not provide any insight as to whether the subsequent outcome merely confirms the banks' expectations or was the result of them.

As well as whether they found their banks supportive, non-supportive or neutral, owners were asked about the frequency with which they saw their bank managers and whether they did so only when requested. Advice from bank managers represents a means of supplementing the volume of human capital available to a small firm. Additionally, a close and willing relationship may facilitate loans that are more readily available or which are provided on more favourable terms.

Table 5.1 Factors associated with survival in construction

High importance	*Less importance*
Age of owner	Proportion of workforce having served an internal apprenticeship
Education of owner (probably!)	Proportion unskilled (negatively)
Proportion of workforce that is skilled	Taking external legal advice on contracts
Employing financial information in decision-making	Ploughing back profits into business
Paying bills promptly	Having a positive reason for starting the business

Table 5.2 Logit regression of survival*

$$22.2444 - 0.5457X_3 + 3.2917X_{73} - 6.7045X_{25} - 2.3562X_{40} - 3.1922X_{83} + 0.1943X_{77}$$

(12.7)	(0.3)	(1.8)	(3.6)	(1.2)	(1.8)	(0.09)
0.08	0.06	0.06	0.05	0.06	0.07	0.03

**R² = 0.84

	0	1	
0	26	2	
1	1	29	overall 95%

X_3 = Age when business started or taken over by present owner
X_{73} = Accountant paid to give advice on tax
X_{25} = Financial advice produced primarily to satisfy Inland Revenue
X_{40} = Number of weeks on average taken to pay bills

Table 5.2 (continued)

X_{83} = Educational level of owner was limited to GCSE/O level or equivalent

X_{77} = Percentage of workers that were skilled tradesmen

---

* When regressions were run on sub-samples of forty-eight observations the coefficients and respective standard errors were:

A) $\quad$ 19.9 – $\quad$ 0.5448 X_3 + $\quad$ 3.58806 X_{73} – $\quad$ 5.5495 X_{25} – $\quad$ 2.2624 X_{40} – $\quad$ 3.4408 X_{83} + $\quad$ 0.1825 X_{77}

$\quad\quad$ (11.2) $\quad\quad$ (0.27) $\quad\quad$ (1.8) $\quad\quad$ (2.9) $\quad\quad$ (1.1) $\quad\quad$ (1.9) $\quad\quad$ (0.08)

B) $\quad$ 12.9945 – $\quad$ 0.7129 X_3 + $\quad$ 5.9072 X_{73} – $\quad$ 5.632 X_{25} – $\quad$ 2.3154 X_{40} – $\quad$ 2.5491 X_{83} + $\quad$ 0.1929 X_{77}

$\quad\quad$ (15.3) $\quad\quad$ (0.33) $\quad\quad$ (2.5) $\quad\quad$ (2.7) $\quad\quad$ (1.2) $\quad\quad$ (1.9) $\quad\quad$ (0.10)

** R^2 = likelihood ratio index = $1 - \dfrac{\text{log likelihood at convergence}}{\text{log likelihood at zero}}$

Standard errors in brackets. Third line refers to level of significance.

RESULTS

(Table 5.1 provides a summary, Table 5.2 the full regression results.) To reiterate, the methodology employed in this study enabled the group of variables to be identified that was most important in distinguishing survivors from failures but does not provide any indication as to whether a particular variable not included in this group nevertheless has some importance. As with most studies based on statistical analysis the assumption is made that correlation implies something about causation. Relationships may be purely a matter of chance, though, on the whole, they remained robust regardless of whether they were applied to the full sample of companies or to randomly selected sub-samples. The reasons behind a relationship can only remain a matter of conjecture though, hopefully, one can make a pretty shrewd guess as to what this might be.

Age

The age at which owners established or took over their companies was strongly and negatively associated with whether their companies survived. Owners of surviving companies were almost always younger than those of failures.

This is somewhat surprising. If people gain in knowledge, experience and levels of skill as they become older then, following Jovanovic, one would expect these increases in the volume of their human capital to lessen the probability of their companies failing. The relationship would be the opposite from that suggested by the results of this study.

It could be that there are disadvantages from age when running a company. Perhaps young people are more open to new ideas; possibly they will possess more determination to succeed; they will probably have more energy.

Whatever the nature of the advantages possessed by the younger owners they would appear to be sufficiently powerful to outweigh those associated with age.

Education

Following Bates (1990) and, to some extent, Jovanovic (1982), one might have expected a strong positive relationship between the education level of owners and the probability of their business surviving, but the results of this study provide only limited support for this hypothesis. First, whereas the regression model run on the full sample would suggest that the owners whose education levels was limited to GCE 'O' level or equivalent or less, the most likely alternatives being HND or City and Guilds certificates, all saw their firms fail, the strength of the relationship was not particularly robust when re-tested on sub-samples of the data. There probably is a relationship but it may be more a matter of chance that it appeared quite as strong as the results would suggest when employing the full sample.

Second, examination of the data reveals that the three owners with degrees all numbered among the failures. This would not be consistent with Bates (op. cit.) who found owners with a college education were more likely to see their firms survive than those less well educated, but it should not be interpreted as a strong refutation of Jovanovic's (op. cit.) learning curve model. Apart from the limited conclusions that can be drawn from such a small sub-sample, his theory did not explicitly state that possession of a degree would necessarily speed progress up the learning curve. Indeed, the pertinent question might be whether the type of human capital embodied in a degree, especially if the degree is non-vocational, is more appropriate for dealing with some sets of market conditions than for others. This must remain an open question.

Skills of the workforce

Human capital is not only embodied in management but in the entire workforce. Perhaps this is the explanation for the clear positive relationship between the probability of survival and the proportion of the workforce that was skilled. Alternatively, the level of skill of its workforce represents a major factor in determining the quality of the products that a firm offers. Generally speaking it is in the interests of a small firm to move upmarket because of the greater scope this offers to add value and compensate for the lower volume which, by most definitions, a small firm must suffer.

Use of information

Owners that produced their financial information primarily to meet their legal requirements towards the Inland Revenue were more likely to see their companies fail than those that employed it in their decision-making. Monitoring what is happening to the revenue and cost streams within a company is clearly of great importance. Indeed, it would appear this has the greatest impact on the probability of survival of the qualitative variables, indicating *yes/no* responses to questions (comparability is less straightforward with the importance of quantitative variables' e.g. age of owner).

Management of cashflow

There would appear to be an inverse relationship between the probability of survival and the time taken to pay bills. This runs counter to the axiom that the later payment is made the better because of the opportunity offered to earn interest in the intervening period and because of the erosion by inflation on the value of the repayments.

One explanation is that firms that are financially healthy are in a better position to pay promptly, though this does not explain why they should choose to do so. Perhaps relationships with suppliers will be enhanced, resulting in quicker delivery, a greater willingness to extend credit during especially difficult circumstances, or preferential treatment in some other respect.

An alternative explanation would be that the difficulties in managing cashflow will become exacerbated if bills are not paid promptly, or at least, if there is no pattern in the length of periods between receipt of bills and their payment. In these circumstances it becomes easy to lose track of unavoidable expenditure and to find one's post dominated by 'final claims'.

Whatever the explanation, it is interesting that Chapter 11 discusses how a quite separate study of the UK instrumentation sector suggested early payment of bills was strongly and positively associated with high rates of profitability.

Other factors

Not only is it possible to identify the variables which would appear to have the strongest influence on the probability of survival of a small construction company but also those which were runners-up in the statistical selection process.

Skill of the workforce

The importance of a commitment to a skilled workforce is confirmed quite strongly by the positive correlation between the probability of survival and the percentage of the workforce that served an internal apprenticeship and the negative correlation with the percentage that was unskilled. It really does seem to matter to small construction firms to employ a high quality workforce, preferably to help its employees to develop that quality.

External advice

Owners that took legal advice when drawing up contracts were more likely to see their firms survive than those who relied solely on their own knowledge of the law. It would seem valuable to supplement from outside sources the volume of human capital available to a firm.

Ploughed back profits

The probability of survival increases with the proportion of profits ploughed back into the running of the business. It is hardly surprising that such an investment represents a safer route to survival than taking profits as personal remuneration but it is perhaps a little surprising that Chapter 3 did not identify any writers who blamed business failure on the preference of owners for instant gratification.

Motivation

Businesses founded through redundancy were more likely to fail than where motivation was more positive. Intuition was confirmed that it is better to want to start a company than to be forced to do so.

Principal components

The attempt to locate groups of factors that were usually found together – principal components as they are technically called – proved singularly unsuccessful and this exercise did not advance our understanding of what distinguishes survivors in construction from failures. However, an interesting insight is provided into one aspect of the population of small construction firms in general. An implication of the lack of correlation between approaches to running a business is that while it may be possible to identify particular management practices which minimize the probability of failure and, therefore, may be fairly described as 'efficient', firms that by this definition are efficient in one respect will not necessarily be efficient in another. Neither would the personal characteristics of owners appear to be reflected in the management practices they adopt. Bearing in mind the crucial caveat that conclusions can only be drawn within the context of the issues addressed, indeed, literally the way the questions were framed, it may be more valid to think in terms of efficient *management practices* than in terms of efficient *management*.

CONCLUDING REMARKS

The construction sector would not be the first choice of a would-be small business person who sought a quiet life, free from the fear of failure. In order to minimize the likelihood that this will occur it helps to be young, though the policy implication that as owners grow older they should devote increasingly more time to diversifying into a safer sector, is clearly easier said than done.

Other conclusions are rather more helpful to owners. It would certainly appear in their interests to employ a skilled workforce or to invest in its training. Equally, they should keep a close eye on their revenue and cost streams.

The results also present some testimony to the importance of taking external advice on legal matters, ploughing back profits into the business rather than taking them immediately as remuneration and of having a fairly positive motive for starting a business. Unfortunately, one must be a little less definitive on the value of education as an antidote to failure.

6

THE PERFORMANCE OF SMALL FIRMS AND OWNER CHARACTERISTICS

The performance of a small firm is here defined as a measure of its success. Given the high fatality rate within the small-firm sector one such measure would be the length of a firm's life. The success of firms that do manage to survive is usually judged in terms of their profitability or growth in sales. This is not unreasonable to the extent that for the majority of owners, other factors remaining equal, an increase in either would be desirable. However, two caveats should be expressed:

1 Though economists will usually assume that owners' sole objective will lie in maximizing their long-term income, which should include remuneration and profits and, arguably, some notion of the change in the value of the firm if it were sold, this is certainly a gross over-simplification. Some owners, for instance, may regard the running of their firm as a remunerative hobby. This might arise if the potential offered by a firm could, realistically, only provide a minor element of the total income received by a household, or if a firm is founded towards the end of an owner's career. At the other end of the spectrum, owners may view their firms as vehicles for self-aggrandisement and aim to make them as large as possible, at the expense of profitability or personal remuneration. They may claim that in the long-term they would expect to see the benefits in higher incomes but this could easily be a rationalization of the process.

2 Included in owners' objectives is their attitude to risk. Much of managerial decision-making consists in taking gambles but just how big a gamble should be taken is clearly a matter of personal preference. When assessing the relative success of the owners of

63

two firms by comparing their incomes, ignoring their attitudes to risk is analogous to ignoring their attitudes to business ethics. The owner with the lower income may not consider the price she perceives the other has paid, in terms of either sleepless nights or unethical behaviour, to have been worth the rewards and, therefore, would regard as unfair the judgement that she were the less successful.

If growth or profitability are accepted as measures of performance, and hence success, identifying the most important factors by which they are influenced represents a truly formidable task. Literally any aspect of a firm can represent such an influence. It is common to divide factors into those relating to the owner, those that are internal to the firm, and those that are external, where internal is defined as being within the firm's control and external as beyond it.[1] This trichotomy implies that the owner is, in a sense, responsible for everything that happens in her firm however trivial or subject to luck – for the breakdown of a fax machine which leads to the loss of a vital order, as much as for the results of a major strategic decision.

It is, however, more realistic to distinguish between the internal and external factors affecting small firms than those affecting large. Small firms may be offered some range of options as to which markets they operate in, in that sense, to face some degree of choice as to an important component of their environment, but once that choice has been made will not be able to alter their environment to anywhere near the extent offered to the majority of large firms. The latter may, for instance, reduce competition through takeovers, and cause major shifts in patterns of demand, and the powers of political lobbying of the biggest, even individually, are likely to be stronger than those of small firms acting collectively through pressure groups. Indeed, at times the influence of the large-firm sector on its environment could truly be described as sinister.

On the other hand, in a small firm the impact of the personal characteristics of the owner may be implanted on all aspects of how it is run, blurring the distinction between personal characteristics and internal factors. In large firms the personal characteristics of chief executives may have only a glancing effect on how they operate and the distinction is correspondingly more legitimate.

This chapter will consider how the personal characteristics of owners might affect performance, other chapters consider various other factors which might do so, drawing on some of the empirical evidence. In attempting to cover such a vast area it would be surprising if some articles of strong relevance were not omitted. This danger arises in all literature reviews but is particularly marked when all studies are based on samples drawn from the small-firm sector. A judgement must be made not only on whether the results of a study are valid with respect to the populations from which the samples are drawn (for instance, road hauliers operating in the north of England or food retailers in Illinois, USA) but whether any conclusions can be drawn with respect to how the performance of small firms operating in other sectors and countries can be improved.

There are four themes running through the literature on the relationship of the personal characteristics of owners to the performance of their firms, though it is not unusual for more than one to be included in the same piece of research. These themes are:

1 The nature of entrepreneurship.
2 The psychology of owners.
3 Types of owners.
4 Backgrounds of owners.

Each will be considered but before doing so a word of caution should be expressed about the methodology employed in the first three. To varying extents they all may be said to involve attempts at establishing the personality of owners, where personality is defined sufficiently broadly to include objectives, values, attitudes and feelings, as well as behaviour in alternative situations. Clearly, this is no mean task and has been approached in a variety of way.[2] For instance, interviewees or respondents (depending on whether information is collected through interviews or a postal survey) may be asked to indicate on a Lickett Scale of 1–5 how far they agree with statements such as 'Managers should not be afraid of putting the interests of the firm before the welfare of society' (The Stratos Group, 1990).

Variations on such an approach, sometimes displaying considerable ingenuity, are common within research in this area. Alternatively, personality might be inferred from owners' accounts of how they managed important events in their companies' histories, or how they would respond to hypothetical situations.

All of the methods have in common the assumption that it is possible to know the link between the information provided and actual personality. This, however, almost verges on an act of faith and for a number of reasons. For instance:

- A very simplistic view of necessity is taken about what constitutes personality. The personality trait displayed by an individual can vary with the situation. The bully at work may be bullied at home. Researchers on personality must assume that the 'side' owners display in a research situation is identical to that displayed when running their firms.

- Interviewees or respondents may be providing a view of themselves in which they would like to believe but which might represent pure self-deception. Casual empiricism, for example, would suggest a distinct lack of correlation between the vehemence with which senior decision-makers in all walks of life espouse the need for participative management and the actual degree of authoritarianism that they display. They may, however, genuinely believe that they are willing to take heed of the views of their subordinates.

- Whereas there may be a relationship between the information provided under research conditions and the personality being studied assumptions about its nature can only be verified by some measure of behaviour. It cannot be emphasized too strongly that attitudes, beliefs and everything else that goes on inside an owner's mind is of no relevance to our understanding of the influences on the performance of his company unless it is reflected in some way by his behaviour.

The problem of assuming a straightforward relationship arizes, as with the above reasons, from the complexity of personality. Take as an example an attitude survey administered to a group of academics and to a group of prison inmates. The former may well appear to be the more understanding of what leads to crime, to be more liberal in their attitudes to punishment. The latter may well display an intolerance to crime that would appear inconsistent with their own behaviour. In this case there is a fairly unambiguous verification measure which is usually absent in the studies which attempt to classify owners by their responses to similar surveys and hence to predict their behaviour in various management situations.

In spite of this scepticism about the methodology employed in the psychological studies of owners the results of such studies have not been omitted from this book. They represent an important tradition in the literature on small firms and many eminent academics would regard the views just expressed as demonstrating an unwarranted harshness, particularly unfair considering the fallibility of other social sciences.

ENTREPRENEURSHIP

It would be difficult to review the literature on the influences on the performance of small firms without including some mention of entrepreneurialism. What is very striking is the contrast between the frequency with which 'entrepreneur' appears and the lack of consensus as to its definition.[3] Sometimes it is used interchangeably with owner–manager. At others, it is used to describe a certain type of owner–manager. Commonly, entrepreneurs are characterized as:

- Willing to take risks, both in the sense of degree of uncertainty in which the business gamble is taken and of the size of the penalty from making the wrong decision.[4]
- A tendency to be innovative, to make changes in the products or services offered, markets served, methods of management, indeed, in most aspects of running her company except, perhaps, in ways that would dilute her personal power.
- The instinctive search for new opportunities and energy to try to exploit them.

Writers may go much further in the attributes they attach to entrepreneurs. Olson (1987), for instance, believed they needed 'patience and the ability to take the long view' as well as 'high tolerance for ambiguous, unstructured situations' and to be 'both intuitive and analytical'.

Kets de Vries (1977) offers the most extreme attempt at generalization about the make-up of entrepreneurs:

> Thus due to the frustrations and perceived deprivations experienced in the early stages of life, a prominent pattern among entrepreneurs appears to be a sense of impulsivity, a persistent feeling of dissatisfaction, rejection and pointlessness, forces which contribute to an impairment and depreciation of his sense of self-esteem and affect cognitive processes. The entrepreneur is a man under great stress, continuously badgered by his past, a past which is experienced and re-experienced in fantasies, daydreams and dreams. These dreams and fantasies often have a threatening content due to the recurrence of feelings of anxiety and guilt which mainly revolve around hostile wishes against parental figures or, more generally, all individuals in a position of authority...
>
> (Kets de Vries 1977: 49)

There is much more in this mode.

Elsewhere (Kets de Vries, 1985) the author lists attributes such as 'need for control', 'sense of distrust' and 'need for applause'.

Hardly surprisingly their personality is extremely unstable!

Other writers on the psychological make-up of entrepreneurs, however defined, have been less prepared to adopt such a broad brush and rather more to measure the relative importance of various personality traits through empirical research. Those that focused on the differences between successful and unsuccessful entrepreneurs, rather than on entrepreneurs in general, will be considered in the next section.

PSYCHOLOGY OF OWNERS

Studies of how the psychology of owners can affect the performance of their firms usually involve putting some sort of test, in the manner described above, to samples of successful and unsuccessful owners and trying to identify any differences. An alternative, adopted by Khan (1986), was to ask venture capitalists to select the personal characteristics they would regard as important for the success of new ventures and then to rate owners of small businesses accordingly. The characteristics were of the sort: 'desire for success', 'tenacity/courage', 'creativity/ingenuity'. When these ratings were employed in a statistical model to explain performance, creativity/ingenuity appeared to do best whereas tenacity/courage was actually negatively related.

Begley and Boyd (1986; 1987) adopted a more common methodology by including a Jenkins Activity Survey in their questionnaires sent to members of the Small Business Association of New England. This was designed to locate respondents within the dimensions of competitiveness, speed and impatience, and job involvement. None of these emerged as particularly important in influencing performance, though 'hard-driving competitiveness' might have had some influence on growth, though their results hinted that if there are stronger relationships, they may not be straightline but more complex.

A similar lack of success in relating personality to performance was exhibited by Rice and Lindecamp (1989) who used a Myers-Briggs test on a sample of Mississippi retailers to assess their personality within the types defined by Jung, that varied according to whether extrovert/introvert, sensitive/intuitive, thinking/feeling, perceiving/judging.

Miller and Toulouse (1986a; b) concentrated on whether owners of Quebec small- to medium-sized enterprises were 'flexible' or 'inflexible': 'The former being "informal, adventurous, confident, humorous, rebellious, idealistic, assertive and egoistic"... highly concerned with personal pleasure and diversion' and whether their 'locus of control' was 'internal' or 'external'. The former 'believe the consequences of his behaviour stem from his efforts ... are more task oriented ... function best in stress ... prefer to be persuaded than coerced'.

Their results have most significance for choice of strategy, which will be considered later, but it is pertinent here that there is some suggestion that flexible owners achieved the best results in stable but not dynamic environments.

Perry, Meredith and Cunnington (1988) attempted to establish whether there was any relationship between the personality of Australian nursery owners and the performance of their companies. Their results suggest that the 'need to achieve', as measured by nAch (McClelland, 1961) and internal locus of control, as defined in the last study, might be correlated with the success of a company during its start-up phase but will not affect growth afterwards.

The results of the most comprehensive study of personality-performance relationships have been reported by McClelland (1986), one of the pioneers in this area. In this study the personality traits were compared of thirty-six 'average' and thirty-six 'superior' small business owners in India, Malawi and Ecuador. These traits were identified through owners' accounts of critical events in their companies' history and how they were managed. Those that were associated with success were apparently being proactive, achievement-orientated and committed (e.g. as reflected by recognizing the importance of business relationships). Those apparently not associated with success included self-confidence, persistence, powers of persuasion or their use of influence.

TYPES OF OWNERS

Related to attempts at identifying the psychological factors associated with success is the notion that owners can be categorized by a mixture of psychological profile, background and behaviour. Categories differ between studies but one commonly identified is that of 'craftsman' or some similar title. In Smith's (1967) classic work they were described as having working-class origins, low or narrow education, successful work records but lack of identification with the senior management in their previous employers. They were paternalistic with employees, their marketing tended to rely on personal relationships and their strategic thinking was rather rigid. These were contrasted with opportunistic entrepreneurs: middle-class, better education, more proactive and taking a wider view of sources of finance and possible feasible strategies. The latter category experienced the higher rates of growth.

The craftsman in Filley and Aldag's (1978) study were non-adaptive, risk-averse, and aimed for a comfortable living rather than the highest possible level of performance. Alternatives to craftsmen were 'promotion' and 'administrative' firms. The former were established to exploit some unique competitive advantage, were informally controlled by the chief executive and were often fairly short-lived. Administrative firms, usually the largest in size, depended less than the other two on the personal leadership of the chief executive, and were more formally organized through written plans and budgetary controls. Again craftsmen performed least well.

Broadly consistent with these results are those of Lafuente and Salas (1989) who contrasted craftsmen with owners that were 'risk-oriented', 'family oriented' and 'managerial'. Levels of performance, as perceived by respondents, were highest with managerial and risk-oriented owners.

A study drawing on a sample of over 1800 small businesses in the USA (Dunkelberg and Cooper, 1982) categorized owners, according to their responses to statements about their goals, into 'orientated towards growth', 'desire for independence' and 'craftsmen orientation', the last defined as 'most comfortable in selling or handling technical problems rather than working on management issues'. Casual inspection of their tables (the usual tests of statistical significance were apparently not applied) does not suggest particularly strong differences between categories in the backgrounds of the owners, none between the growth (in employment) displayed by growth- and independence-orientated owners, though the craftsmen probably performed least well, and very little, if any, in the income they received from their businesses.

If there are different categories of small business owner it would seem possible, therefore, to over-simplify the nature of the differences between them. This conclusion is reinforced by Hornaday and Wheatley (1986) who found differences in performance within the categories suggested by Filley and Aldag (1978), rather than between them, reflecting differences in the growth orientation of owners within the same categories.

The results of the last papers notwithstanding, it is plausible that the education levels and class origins of owners will influence their career patterns before starting their own businesses and this, in turn, will affect the choice of activity that is open to them. On average, one would expect the better educated, and middle-class to be better equipped to undertake the most promising activities. It would not be surprising if their responses to questionnaires suggested they were the more ambitious, because people will generally adjust their aspirations to match what can reasonably be expected. What is left as an open question from the research so far is whether growth orientation will differ between people from different backgrounds but facing identical opportunities.

BACKGROUND OF OWNERS

Apart from attempts at identifying categories of owners, such as craftsmen *et al.*, there is a limited literature[5] on the backgrounds of owner–managers, with a few articles on the features distinguishing high performers from low. Cooper (1985) focused on the 'incubators' – previous employers – of owners of a sample of American high growth firms and found 84 per cent had been located in the same geographical area; that 64 per cent were in related businesses, which dropped to 41 per cent when high technology companies (as might operate in computers, software and biotechnology), were excluded; 77 per cent came from another business, rather than a university, which would not have been surprising in a European context, but, interestingly, in the biotechnology and medical sectors, only 41 per cent. Unfortunately, in the absence of a control group it is not possible to draw any conclusions about whether these statistics provide any insights into the factors associated with success or simply of small firms in general.

For the backgrounds of successful British owners of small firms the best accounts have been provided by Storey, Watson and Wynarczyk (1989), which compared the characteristics of twenty fast-growth companies and their owners from the north-east of England with a control group matched by start-up date and sector. Regarding the owners of the fast-growth companies it would appear that they were:

- More likely to explain their decision to start a business in terms of 'pull' factors, such as market opportunity, than 'push' factors such as unemployment.

- Better qualified in terms of school and sub-degree qualifications.
- Possibly more likely to have been previously employed in the same sector.
- More likely to have had management experience.
- Possibly more likely to have been employed in a medium-sized firm.

There was no obvious difference between the two groups in their experience of owning companies or in their average age.

In a separate study, based on a much larger sample drawn from the Cleveland area, Storey and Strange (1992), allowed some conclusions to be drawn about influences on profitability, rather than growth. Their results confirmed that staying in the same sector might benefit performance, but suggested that previous management or ownership experience did not make any difference; if anything the last would appear to have affected performance detrimentally.

CONCLUDING REMARKS

The views expressed in this chapter on the problems associated with attempts at linking the characteristics of owners, in particular those relating to their personality, with the ways that they manage their companies and, hence, levels of performance that they achieve, are highly contentious and would not be received with very much sympathy by many eminent researchers. They might well argue, with good reason, that it is an area too important to be ignored, and that its methodological shortcomings are no worse than when addressing other questions within the social sciences, though the nature of the shortcomings may differ. Economists are commonly accused, for instance, of displaying a misplaced faith in the reliability of 'hard' data, that can be readily measured or identified, especially if derived from secondary sources, which assumes a degree of objectivity which closer examination may reveal to be unwarranted.

It is certainly true that it is easier to define and carry out empirical research on such personal characteristics as age, education and previous management experience than on personality. This is the practical reason for the scant award in this book to the latter rather than from any belief that owner personality has no impact on the management of a small firm.

7

STRATEGIC PLANNING AND THE SMALL FIRM

Strategy is about the major moves made by a firm. Marketing strategy involves choice of markets, positioning within them, broad approaches to confronting or exploiting the various elements that constitute a market. It is common to write as if marketing issues alone constituted strategy but decisions to replace permanent sales staff by freelancers, to introduce full automation and to go public, might be described as, respectively, elements of personnel, manufacturing and financial strategy.

One can argue about where the line should be drawn between strategy and tactics – presumably it is not always clear-cut in even a military context – but clearly all firms undertake strategy, whether or not they would use the term to describe what they were doing. The owner of a corner shop must make decisions about its location, product lines, hours of opening and prices, all of which are elements of strategy. Naturally, decisions can be taken by default. If it never occurs to the owner that she could move her business, or change what she were selling, both unlikely possibilities, a decision, nevertheless, has in a sense still been made, albeit unconsciously.

Writers on strategy usually concentrate on answering one of the following:

- By what processes within a firm is strategy determined?
- What should be this process in order to achieve the most success?
- What strategies should it be pursuing?

Although these questions spring from different traditions it is, in fact, difficult to provide prescriptions for the second without being at least aware of the sort of descriptive answers that might be provided to the first. Indeed, increasingly, strategists are recognizing the importance of strategic processes to the formulation of optimal strategies.

This chapter will discuss the process of strategy, whereas Chapter 8 will present first principles, Chapter 9 will consider the relationship of market structure to performance, and Chapter 10 will discuss the validity of organization lifecycle models.

THE STRATEGIC PROCESS

Organizations will differ in the degree to which they are formalized. The army, with its unambiguous hierarchy, decision-making systems set down in manuals and strategies and battle plans which are spelled out in detail on paper, represents an organization in which the formal dimension of decision-making plays an important part. In a small firm the only formality may be in the yearly accounts and even these may owe as much to the ingenuity of an accountant as to the reality of the firm's finances.

The question of relevance to the purposes of this book is whether increasing the degree of formality by introducing formal planning would improve the performance of the small firm. For many writers on planning it is self-evident that it would. For Scarborough and Zimmerer (1987) 'Developing a strategic plan is critical to the creation of a small company's critical edge' and 'defines what a company will be'.

The constituents of such a plan would be:

- A clear mission statement.
- The collection and assimilation of all relevant information.
- A hierarchy of goals and objectives governing all levels of the firm.
- The formulation of options and selection of optimal strategies.
- Translation of plans into actions.
- An accurate control mechanism to monitor progress and to indicate remedial action where appropriate.

The most comprehensive guide to the components of successful corporate planning for firms in general, rather than for small in particular, is provided by Argenti (1985). Though he is at pains to emphasize that the

> corporate plan is seen today as a simple statement reflecting a consensus among the top few people in an organization concerning the few things that these top executives believe that their company, as a corporate whole, has to get right over the follow-

ing years ... to obtain a consensus among the top few people in an organization regarding its very destiny. . .

which would imply it is intended for use in large firms, the 'deliberately methodical approach' that he proposes would represent an excellent blueprint for all those who would advocate the use of planning by all firms, large and small alike:

- Set corporate objectives and targets.
- Forecast performance in key areas comparing predictions with targets to assess the 'size of the strategic task that lies ahead'.
- Assess strengths and weaknesses.
- Assess threats and opportunities.
- Generate alternative strategies.
- Decide on the appropriate strategy.
- Evaluate whether this really is the right decision.
- Develop action and business plans.
- Monitor progress.

Proponents of formal planning see little need to debate whether it really does produce the benefits they would claim. These are self-evident in a world in which data will be rationally assessed and strategies chosen objectively to achieve the goals set by the chief executive. Discussion with the (loyal) workforce will probably prove sufficient to achieve consensus about the need for the strategy. In any case, careful monitoring, by implication supported by sticks and carrots, will ensure compliance. There are, however, powerful arguments why faith may be misplaced in what Henry Mintzberg,[1] its most cogent critic, terms the 'Planning School' of strategy (Mintzberg, 1990), or, at least, the perceived benefits exaggerated:

- Some strategic moves may be made 'deliberately', to quote Mintzberg, through a formal process. Others 'emerge' from within the organization. The latter may simply reflect developments, benign or malign, internal or external to the organization, that had not been foreseen in the grand plan, or the process may be demonstrating the importance of the informal side of an organization, the side that does not appear on paper but results from culture, which is itself the end-product of history, shared experiences and organizational gut feeling about what is right. Such considerations become more relevant for small firms as they grow older and bigger; until then, it is usually more appropriate to think in terms of the psychology of their owners. Miller and Toulouse (1986a, b) argue that personality will have the greatest impact on the strategies pursued by small firms operating in 'unstable' environments, because stability will tend to produce a greater degree of conformity in behaviour. They claim their survey of Quebec small business people suggests that flexible chief executives (presumably usually owners) would be more likely to employ a niche strategy, rely on intuition for key decisions and to structure their organizations informally.

- Even where strategies appear to have been deliberate, cultural and psychological influences may affect the rationality of the process. Equally for MBAs employed in the central planning department of a multinational, or the owner of a small firm struggling to formulate a viable plan, perceptions are rarely completely objective on factors such as the nature of competition, state of demand or quality of products. Lack of objectivity leads to data being sculptured accordingly. An apparently rational process may be nothing more than a rationalization of beliefs. Formal planning may serve as a legitimation of intuition.

- This is not to disparage intuition. When Mintzberg (Campbell, 1991) extolled its virtues he was probably thinking of large firms but it is even more important for small. The prerequisite of all planning is that the future can be forecast or, at least, the combinations of events constituting alternative scenarios.[2] Unfortunately, not only will a myriad of factors affect the results of an event but the future behaviour of these factors and their relationship to the event will largely remain uncertain, in the sense that the probabilities will be unknown. This would be true even when making forecasts of aggregate demand for a product, the trend of which displays an element of stability over time. Self-evidently it would be so with respect to forecasting the behaviour of competitors. Decision-making in business may be compared to playing roulette simultaneously on numerous roulette wheels without knowing the number of pockets on each one.

Fortunately, the uncertainty of business can usually be condensed into a limited number of decisions, which can be resolved by judgement with as much likelihood of being sound as the results of pseudo-scientific analysis:

- An essential component of formal planning is a clear statement of goals from the chief executive which, in turn, will be translated into a series of goals and targets for the constituent elements within the firm. The goal of any organization will be a weighted average of the goals of its members and other stakeholders able to influence its behaviour, with the weights equal to the power to enforce their goals. The goals of the firm will be synonymous with those of the chief executive to the extent that the latter has the power to enforce his goals and to the extent that there is congruence about goals between him and the members and stakeholders of his firm.

The owner of a small firm is very likely to possess the power to make her goals synonymous with those of her firm. Where she shares ownership, her co-owners will probably possess similar goals. Compare this to power struggles within any large corporation, where chief executives, each senior manager, the labour force, and the shareholders may be pulling in different directions and each possesses some measure of power to affect the eventual outcome. Small wonder if the way that the company behaves bears only a passing resemblance to what was originally envisaged in the corporate plan.

To the extent that small firms are characterized by an absence of such power struggles, formally expressed goals will be more likely to be translated into actual behaviour. It is still not clear, however, why the owners of small firms should expect to achieve any benefits from writing down what they are attempting to achieve. The importance of goals as fundamental driving forces, such as income, growth or social status, will not be enhanced by committing them to paper. Perhaps it will prove more helpful to write down the objectives of strategies that are intended to achieve these goals: 'to provide the best customer service', 'the highest quality products', 'to be the market leader in Glasgow', but supposing that these do not turn out to be the most appropriate means to achieve the *raison d'être* of the organization? They will either be abandoned, in which case they were irrelevant, or if adhered to, will act as disfunctional straightjackets. This is probably why mission statements, which fashion once dictated as indispensable prerequisites for successful strategy formulation, are characterized by their blandness.

The arguments for and against formal planning rest, to a large extent, on the view that is taken of how decisions are made in organizations. Even its critics, however, may be prepared to accept some of its benefits:

- Operational planning, which is concerned with implementation of decisions, rather than their formulation, may be improved from some degree of system, simply because of the sheer volume of information involved. This, no doubt, explains the plethora of user-friendly software designed to assist in operational planning. It is, perhaps, not without significance that strategic planning software is much rarer.

- Even intuition can be aided by committing the choices to paper and spelling out in detail what might be involved. It probably works for some kinds of minds and not for others.

- Formal plans may well be required to satisfy providers of finance, even if the level of hard analysis behind projections of costs and revenues is rather low.

- Senior management, may fully acknowledge the difficulty in formal planning, especially as regards the uncertainty of outcomes to decisions, but argue that it would be unconscionable simply to rely on hunches for proaction or to be caught completely by surprise by changes in circumstances. Casual empiricism would suggest that this is an attitude particularly favoured by planners in large companies. Decision-makers in small firms are less likely to take this 'comfort-rag' approach to formal planning and to be more relaxed about relying on quick response for exploiting opportunities and avoiding threats.

VALUE OF STRATEGIC PLANNING: THE EVIDENCE

Attempts at establishing empirically the value of strategic planning to small firms, mostly based on American data, usually consist of asking their owners whether they carry this out, and if so, how, the areas of activity it covers, and then looking for correlations with performance, often by dividing samples into high and low performers and trying to identify any differences. Such an approach would not be untypical of research into other areas of management but is plagued with weaknesses. Owners may be reluctant to admit they do not plan formally in case it reflects badly on their competitiveness, or they may misinterpret the questions or not understand them at all. These dangers are heightened when information is collected through postal surveys rather than personal interviews, and to their number is added the dilemma of non-response; is it safe to assume the only difference between respondents and non-respondents is that the former bothered to return the questionnaire, whereas the latter did not? In management research the endemic fear is that the answer to this is usually in the negative, either because not being able to find the time to fill in a questionnaire may be a symptom of inefficiency in general or because non-respondents believe their management practices, especially if lacking in sophistication, may be judged critically by researchers.

In spite of the possible bias, in particular from the last reason, towards producing an exaggerated impression of how much formal planning is undertaken by small firms, it does not appear to be particularly prevalent. This would certainly be the conclusion to be drawn from the celebrated review of the literature by Robinson and Pearce (1984), who ascribe its absence to reasons such as lack of time and expertise rather than its irrelevance to sound decision-making. Carland, Carland and Carroll (1989), when finding only sixty-four, of 368 founders of small firms, claimed to use formal written plans, and over 100 admitted to no planning of any kind, looked for links with the characteristics of owners. Formal planners were described as 'entrepreneurs', scoring highly on measures of innovativeness, need for achievement and risk-taking; non-planners were simply 'owner–managers'. Pelham and Clayson (1988) did not make such implied criticism of non-planners but argued the owners of small firms generally found frequent changes to operating plans to be more helpful than reliance on formal planning.

The evidence is mixed on whether small firms that do plan formally achieve higher levels of performance than those that do not. Not only do results differ between studies but sometimes the data presented in individual studies does not offer scope for drawing firm conclusions, with matters made worse by the lack of statistical rigour displayed within much of the research, the reason given by Robinson and Pearce (*op. cit.*) for their rather equivocal interpretation of the evidence. This would, no doubt, be an unduly harsh comment on the methodology employed by Ackelsberg and Arlow (1985) but, in spite of the title of their well-known paper, *Small Businesses Do Plan and It Pays Off,* their results offer mixed testimony to the benefits of formal planning. Whereas the average growth, and to a lesser extent, the change in profits, was higher for planners than non-planners, there was no correlation of either measure with the degree of formality displayed and only a weak correlation of change in profits with the authors' measure of analytical sophistication; the correlation with growth was higher, however. When the results are broken down by sectors there is no statistically significant relationship between measures of either aspect of planning – formality and analysis – and change in profits and a strong negative relationship in manufacturing between degree of formality and growth in sales.

Orpen (1985) did not find any correlation between the time devoted, as reflected by diary entries, to long-range planning and growth or return on assets, but there is some suggestion that these measures were related to two aspects of formal planning. 'High performers' were apparently more likely to establish planning committees and consultations with 'specific individuals' were more likely before major planning decisions were made. Unfortunately, the paper is too vague on important details to be regarded as particularly helpful.

Shrader, Mulford and Blackburn (1989), though arguing that formal planning 'forces ideas and objectives to be thought out', could only find odd correlations, usually weak, of certain aspects of planning with performance in various years and certainly no strong overall relationship.

Writers who unambiguously do not find formal planners achieved superior results are Robinson and Pearce (1983) in their study of South Carolina banks, Cragg and King (1988) who found a negative relationship within their sample of British metal goods manufacturers and Shuman, Shaw and Sussman (1985) who found no relationship within America's 500 fastest-growing privately held companies. The authors found it:

> Particularly interesting that 95.5 per cent of those without a business plan are operating at a profit in comparison to 84.1 per cent with a business plan, with 30.0 per cent of those without a business plan having profits in excess of 16 per cent versus 19.8 per cent of the ones with business plans having similar profits.

Turning to writers whose results are more positive in their support for the benefits of formal planning, Schwenk and Shrader (1993) in their comprehensive review of the literature to date cleverly pooled the results of various different studies to conclude that planning did have a small but positive relationship with performance. Other writers, such as Bracker and Pearson (1986), found that south-eastern American dry cleaners who carried out 'structured strategic' planning achieved higher levels of sales and 'entrepreneurial compensation' (net profits + owner manager compensation) than those employing types of planning that were regarded as of lower levels of sophistication but there were no differences in performance within groups of firms employing types at lower levels. Firms with over five years of planning history, though, out-performed those with less than five in terms of sales growth but not entrepreneurial compensation.

In a study of the electronics sector employing similar categories of planning the same authors (Bracker, Keats and Pearson, 1988) found structured strategic planners continued to achieve higher levels of growth and income growth than other types of planners with, again, no difference between the latter. When the sample was broken down into types of owners those defined as 'opportunistic' gained all the benefits from structured decision-making but 'craftsmen' did not. This is a curious result because type of owner did not appear to be related to performance. Length of planning history did not appear to make any difference to performance.

CONCLUDING REMARKS

Formal strategic planning would not appear to be particularly common among small firms but neither is the evidence overwhelmingly persuasive that this is to be regretted. The complexity that can arise in operations management may make highly desirable the commitment of the details to paper but strategic issues are usually fairly simple, though surrounded by uncertainty, and written plans may be largely an irrelevancy to their resolution. For some owners of small firms formal planning is a help, if only because of the comfort it provides that something is being done. It is more a matter of what is right for them than of a sound management practice that should always be adopted.

8

FIRST PRINCIPLES OF STRATEGY

Underlying much of Mintzberg's writing is a scepticism about the value of producing general prescriptions about the strategies that should be adopted to exploit or cope with particular situations. Among his arguments would be that firms should decide for themselves what is right for them in the light of their experience, traditions, culture and organizational structure and should avoid adopting mechanistic formulas.

This book is written on the premise that two sources of guidance can, at least, prove helpful in strategy formulation though it is fully accepted that they can only be complements to detailed knowledge of an industry. The first of these sources would be a theoretical framework based, for the most part, on economics. This enables the most appropriate strategies to be identified to meet specific conditions, other factors remaining equal. Only in extreme conditions will omitted factors prove so important as to render theory totally redundant, though certainly it may need to be modified. The second source would be the results of empirical studies of the relationship between strategy and performance. Firms can only gain from a knowledge of which strategies would appear to have had the strongest correlations with levels of performance whatever the processes by which they were formulated. Of course, firms may choose to dismiss these relationships as irrelevant to their circumstances, and their judgement may be perfectly correct, but they would be very foolish to reach this decision without first examining why it should be so. Indeed the very act of carrying out this examination could, in itself, be a salutary exercise.

Chapters 11 and 12 present the results of two empirical studies. The explanation they contain of the choice of variables will of necessity involve some reference to theory. This chapter will present the first principles of economic strategy, which represent a useful starting point for an understanding of how small firms might formulate their strategies.

FIRST PRINCIPLES

The total volume of profits earned by a firm will be determined by how much it sells, its costs and its prices. Normally performance is defined in terms of profitability, the ratio of profits to some indication of size, usually value of assets or sales, though what is theoretically the most appropriate is the subject of a debate which, thankfully, is beyond the scope of this book.

Profitability is of interest to the owner of a small firm if she were comparing its rate of return with that from alternative investments or if she were making an assessment of its efficiency compared to other businesses. It might well also affect its sale price. However, it is the total profits of the firm which represents the potential maximum total income – at least if the question is avoided of how much should be ploughed back to fund investment – that it could afford to pay her and which may, therefore, be of more importance. Certainly casual empiricism would suggest that owners of small firms are more likely to know their previous year's total profits than profitability.

Although it is not particularly profound to decompose profits into their three elements the implications of this trichotomy are not trivial for the formulation of strategy. If nothing else changes detrimentally in the process, increased profits will result from growth in sales, reductions in costs and increases in prices. Strategies that are intended to increase profits can only do so through one of these routes.

Growth

Strategies intended to achieve growth unfortunately usually cannot be achieved without some cost. Increasing market-share within established markets may involve price cutting, increases in advertising expenditure or in the size of the sales force. Untapped markets will often remain untapped until expenditure has been undertaken. Expenditure will be required to secure an increase in demand and then to meet that demand. Whereas increases in the efficiency of businesses enable them to achieve differences in throughput times which, to all intents and purposes, may be regarded as costless, generally expansion in sales can only be achieved through an increase in the amount of resources employed. These two sources of increased expenditure, to secure expansion in both demand and production, are reasons why growth may lead to increases in total profits but no change or a decrease in profitability and, in the worst scenarios, can result in a fall in the total profits that a firm actually earns.

For the owner of a small company considering whether to attempt to increase the size of his company the issue is how the costs of doing so will move in relation to the benefits. In the dismal world, often used as a starting point for theoretical analysis in economics, it is difficult for a firm to secure a long-term advantage because of the competitive markets in which it purchases its resources. Whatever option is open to one firm will be open to another. It is straightforward to depict the consequences in markets occupied by a few large firms. If one firm undertakes a price war or an advertising campaign to increase its market-share what is there to stop its competitors from doing the same? As long as there are above normal profits to be earned it will be in the firms' interests to continue to adopt some or other measure to increase demand: to cut prices, for instance, or, increase expenditure on advertising. Eventually the size of the price cut or increase in advertising expenditure would rise to equal its benefits from doing so. Firms will not, of course, be able to react instantaneously. It takes time to formulate new strategies, mobilize resources or purchase new ones. Hence, in the short-term competitive advantage may be secured. Similarly, there may be differences in the quality in the resources employed. A firm may mount a particularly successful sales campaign or be run by an unusually gifted manager, but traditionally economists would ask whether the former could be sustained in the long-term and would ask whether market forces would not eventually force the rise in the salary of the latter to equal the benefits from her brilliance.

To be fair to economists, especially those specializing in business strategy, the above framework is often only a launching pad into the world of reality. Examinations of such issues as whether a firm should move first, or should wait until a competitor has 'tested the water', or, indeed, of the degree that firms face real strategic choices, would be largely irrelevant in this framework. Some economists are even becoming aware of the significance of culture to the determination of strategy.

In summary, other things remaining equal, large firms operating in, and purchasing their resources from, markets which are competitive, will be forced, in the long-term, to spend amounts on the acquisition of market-share equal to the benefits from its increase. Other things will not, however, always remain equal. Of pertinence to the purposes of this book is whether the same can be said of the small-firm sector.

If the resources employed by a small firm are supplied under competitive conditions then they will be equally available to its competitors. It may be able to achieve an advantage but it will prove short-lived. Perhaps its strategic management will consist of continually staying one step ahead of the opposition, which is how the owners of small firms often describe their situation.

This may be overly pessimistic. A small firm may possess some sort of advantage which enables it to grow without seeing this advantage matched by its competitors or the benefits from increased size eroded by competitive pressure until they equal the cost of achieving it.

Where small firms must exercise great caution is in being too ready to assume such an advantage. Cases are too numerous to mention of the senior management of large firms, backed by powerful marketing and research teams, deluding themselves that they were somehow able to achieve a devastating long-term blow to their competitors but becoming locked, instead, in a grinding war of attrition. If such self-delusion is possible within large firms, it is certainly possible within small.

One difference that may exist between large and small firms is that the behaviour of the latter is less likely to be monitored by their competitors. If these are large, they may not be bothered to keep a close watch on what is happening among the small firms within their markets. If, on the other hand, their competitors are small, they may not possess the resources to conduct market intelligence. The result might be that attempting to increase market-share might escape the notice of competitors. A cut in prices, or a sales promotion, or redesign of a product, might stand a good chance, therefore, of not acting as a trigger to a series of counter-moves and counter-counter-moves, reflected in a downward spiral of profits.

Costs

The relationship of cost to levels of output represents one of the most important influences on the formulation of strategy. Small firms are simply denied access to markets, or, more typically, segments of markets, characterized by significant economies of scale, though, as will be discussed below, they will probably be able to carve out niches in segments where cost is not the factor crucial for success.

Though small firms are not able to compete through economies of scale they may be offered the opportunity to exploit economies of scope, that is the advantages, to which brief allusion was made in Chapter 2, from the range of products it offers. Introductory economics text-books invariably depict cost curves as though they were common to all firms but, in fact, the costs to a firm of producing any product, will depend upon the other products it produces. A small firm specializing in manufacturing adult clothing could easily switch its machines to the production of children's clothing at a cost far less than would be incurred by a firm entering clothing production from scratch, yet the adult and children's clothing markets are totally different in their consumers and quite different in the majority of other characteristics. Similarly, a brewer could produce soft drinks at a lower price than a firm of similar size entering the drinks business for the first time.

Economies of scope can affect the shape and position of demand curves as well as that of cost curves. This would occur when consumers are attracted to a product by the reputation that its producers have earned from other products. These could be quite different but usually company reputation can only be exploited where there is some sort of common denominator. A company noted for the quality of its chocolates would experience a higher level of demand if it were to branch into liquorice or candy than if it were new to confectionery but would not enjoy any similar advantage if it were to move into garden products.

A variation on economics of scope in the stimulation of demand would occur where consumers can be persuaded to extend their range of purchases beyond what they had initially intended. Retailers are past masters of exploiting such opportunities, though they have undoubtedly become more imaginative in the breadth of the range they are prepared to sell under one roof. In hypermarkets there may be virtually no consumer products that are not on offer but smaller retailers are increasingly displaying a willingness to sell products that are linked by the situation in which they would be consumed, jams sold in bakers, for instance, or insurance, even suitcases, in travel agents. Indeed, on some occasions garden products could very readily be sold in conjunction with confectionery – chocolate eggs nested in daffodils at Easter, some similar joint merchandising of liqueurs and roses on Mothering Sunday.

The implication of these points is that economies of scope are not excluded to small firms to anywhere near the extent as economies of scale, though the opportunities for such 'cross-pollination' will clearly be limited by the number of products they offer.

Costs are affected by economies of scale and scope. A further source of cost reduction is the knowledge gained by the firm. Over time this will increase with respect to individual managers and other workers, and also collectively within the organization, as embodied in its methods, processes and procedures. Together, individual and collective knowledge constitute corporate knowledge. Increases in knowledge would normally be reflected in lower costs, less uncertainty about cost levels, this being the assumption behind Jovanovich's (1982) model relating the age and size of companies to the probability of failure, and discussed in Chapter 2.

The issues facing the owners of small firms are how increases in such knowledge can be achieved, better equipping them to meet the competition from both small and large firms, and whether large firms enjoy any sort of advantage over small in the accumulation of knowledge. An affirmative response to the latter would represent a further reason why small firms should attempt to operate in market segments unpopulated by firms that are significantly bigger.

Both issues are clouded by the notion of 'experience curves', propounded by the Boston Consulting Group (Boston Consulting Group, 1970 and Henderson, 1974), which for a time was popular within strategic thinking, indeed being employed in the formulation of government policy. Experience curves which related costs, 'all costs (including capital, administrative, research and marketing)', to accumulated output, i.e. to production in the past, were presented as a radical alternative to the economies of scale of traditional micro-economics, which relates costs to current levels of output. Costs:

> decline by some characteristic amount each time accumulated experience is doubled... The characteristic decline is consistently 20 per cent to 30 per cent each time accumulated production is doubled. The decline goes on in time without limit (in constant dollars)... The rate of decline is surprisingly consistent even from industry to industry.

> (Boston Consulting Group, 1970: 12)

Though this decline does depend upon the ability of management to exploit this potential.

The ingredients of the theory of experience curves – the crucial role played by past output, the universality of the costs affected and the constancy of the relationship over time and across sectors – had powerful implications for all firms, regardless of size, particularly as regards the importance of being first to enter production and of building up the amount of experience by producing as much as possible, but particularly for small firms because the only way for a firm to compensate for lack of past output would be to expand its current volume of output. Clearly, large firms can quickly build up their experience, undermining the competitive position of even well established smaller firms.

Fortunately, for the owners of small firms, in its major publication the Boston Consulting Group (*op. cit.*) does not present a shred of direct evidence on cost behaviour, surrogating in its exhibits company cost by industry price, which, as the Boston Consulting Group does not generally expect price to parallel cost, is a rather inappropriate specification. Moreover, the Boston Consulting Group's exposition suggests a certain confusion about the forces underlying experience curves. Elsewhere (Hall and Howell, 1985), the author of this book has commented:

> in a short pamphlet (Henderson, 1974) on the influences under-lying the experience phenomenon, it is claimed that learning will reduce costs by 10–15 per cent as accumulated output is dou-bled; specialization – itself made possible by scale – will reduce them by a further 10–15 per cent and what is acknowledged to be the effect of scale 'alone is sufficient to approximate the experience curve effect where growth is constant and scale grows with volume'.

It would appear, therefore, that experience curves are really little different from conventional economies of scale. This may not be good news for small firms but they do not represent some new source of threat.

The weakness of the arguments presented by the Boston Consulting Group regarding the validity of experience curves does not imply that companies are not able to accumulate knowledge. The notion of learning-by-doing, leading to 'learning curves', is well-established within the work study literature, but only labour costs are affected and it is not accompanied by the hyperbole with which the Boston Consulting Group has surrounded experience curves. What learning and experience curves have in common, however, is the importance they attach to accumulated output. Firms gain in knowledge through production and companies with histories of equal amounts of accumulated output, irrespective of how that output has been distributed over time, will enjoy similar cost levels. This means that established small firms can build up cost advantages over potential entrants without increasing their size but, as the Boston Consulting Group would correctly argue, such advantages can be readily undermined by companies pushing for market-share.

This result, which is rather dismal for small firms, is contingent upon there only being one route by which corporate knowledge can be increased, that is through increased production. Suppose, however, that time plays a part. Certainly elapsed time will affect learning at the level of individual members of the organization. Sudden blasts of information, as innumerable students have found to their cost, are seldom as beneficial as information absorbed more gradually.

The value of collective knowledge will also be enhanced if it is acquired over a period of time. The most appropriate processes and procedures cannot be developed simultaneously; some degree of experimentation is often involved. Trial runs are usually required to smooth out mistakes. The contribution of time might be equally important as accumulated output to the acquisition of corporate knowledge and would be an explanation for the persistence of high performance among long-established small firms, whose expertise sometimes seems to elude much bigger companies.

Corporate knowledge can be gained in ways other than through experience. It can be acquired through general education, management and training courses. It can be acquired through the labour market by recruiting managers and other workers with the required skills. It is true that such skills may not be perfectly transferable because people may only achieve their full potential in a particular kind of culture but, for every talented manager or craftsman who would find a move difficult between the large- and small-firm sectors, there will be another who would find such a move a liberating experience. Skills are mobile within the small-firm sector, though the constraining force may have less to do with adjusting to different cultures as to learning to work with new personalities, especially the owners.

Pricing

Small firms are denied the benefits from economies of scale but may be able to achieve a competitive position by exploiting the opportunities presented by economies of scope and by increasing their volume of corporate knowledge. The principal way, however, that small firms are able to achieve high returns is through the prices that they charge.

In order to understand the process it is useful to regard products as bundles of characteristics or attributes. These can be measurable (the size of a jacket) or objectively classifiable (its colour) or maybe a matter of judgement (the tailoring skills exhibited) and, even more subjective (the image that is projected by the jacket).

Collectively, the amount and nature of its characteristics will determine the total demand for a product. Rather less obviously, its price will be equal to the sum total of the 'shadow prices' of these characteristics, each of which will be determined in a separate market, subject to similar forces to those operating in conventional product markets. The standard components of a jacket – the minimum amount of warmth, comfort and durability – can be readily supplied by any manufacturer and the markets for such components might accurately be described as highly competitive with the implication that there will be little scope for charging a price much above costs.

Companies will be offered the possibility of charging premium prices, incorporating higher than minimum level profits, if they include some feature into their jackets which is different, for instance gold buttons. The amount of profit that the company will earn from so doing will depend upon the demand curve for gold buttons and the length of time it takes for other manufacturers to replace their buttons with gold. There may be some feature that can never be replicated, most obviously brand labels. These bestow a monopoly that can be enjoyed indefinitely but the shadow price that can be charged for the label will depend upon the value that consumers attach to it. Labels may possess no significance for consumers, so that the monopoly it provides generates no additional profits or perhaps consumer loyalty proves fickle and a designer label loses its cachet, with its shadow price displaying a concommitent reduction.

The shadow prices that can be charged for any characteristic will be determined by the elements of the market for that characteristic. Firms not intending to compete on price should supply characteristics the markets for which have the following features:

- Demand is potentially adequate (defined rather loosely in terms of the capacity of the company), or for which demand can be created through marketing.
- Ideally, there should not be other suppliers of the characteristics

but, at least, the number should be sufficiently small to facilitate tacit collusion on the avoidance of a price war.
• Some sort of barriers should make new entry difficult, providing a period during which the potential offered by limited competition can be exploited.

This formula would apply equally to firms of all sizes though small are far less likely to be able to employ the marketing resources to create demand. For all firms it would also be true that most of the characteristics embodied in their products are supplied under competitive conditions with their shadow prices correspondingly low. It is one of the purposes of strategic thinking to identify those characteristics which need not be supplied under such conditions.

There is nothing very insightful about this analysis which is simply considering the markets for characteristics in a similar fashion as is traditional for the markets for products. It does, however, prove helpful in understanding the strategic behaviour of small firms. Take as an example Pakistani restaurants operating in Britain. Unless they choose to concentrate in a part of town associated with Asian restaurants, typically they will be scattered on high streets throughout the city. If they are the only Asian restaurant in that part of town they will possess a local monopoly in the supply of Asian cooking. If there are other types of restaurants in the area the characteristic common to them all – 'eating out' – will be supplied competitively and its shadow price will be lower than if the Pakistani restaurant had been the only restaurant in the area. As it is, the restaurant is only in a position to charge a premium price reflecting consumers' preference for Pakistani food and their unwillingness to travel to the next restaurant selling such food.

If there are two Pakistani restaurants they may decide that there is sufficient demand to warrant them both occupying the same segment of the market, i.e. they would supply the same sets of characteristics. They would then be well advised to agree to avoid cut-throat competition on price, and this agreement could be either overt, in the smoke-filled rooms of business legend, or what was in their joint interest could be tacitly understood. Alternatively, the restaurants could avoid head-to-head competition by offering differing sets of characteristics, one, perhaps, providing an exotic decor and food with subtle tastes whilst another might target late night diners with less refined tastes. These represent two major segments of the markets for Asian food. Simply providing characteristics for which there is no demand would not be enough to guarantee a healthy return. Southern Indian food would be a welcome addition to normal Asian menus but casual empiricism would suggest that UK restaurants specializing in this type of food have not generally proved successful at overcoming the instinctive conservatism among the British about what they are served.

It should be evident from this example that the prices that Pakistani restaurateurs can charge cannot be divorced from the characteristics of their products – ambience, food, opening hours, courtesy of staff, etc. – nor can these characteristics be regarded as independent of the strategies they adopt, because segments of markets are defined in terms of the required characteristics. Whereas it may be normal to distinguish between segments by types of consumer, if these do not differ in some way in the characteristics they require in the product, for all intents and purposes they occupy the same segment. The weakness of this view of segmentation is that to be totally valid, the definition of characteristics would have to be widened to include aspects of marketing such as the image portrayed in advertising messages and channel of distribution as it is possible to segment a market by selling a physically identical product to different types of consumers by varying the methods of marketing as appropriate.

CONCLUDING REMARKS

Even the most basic of economic principles can have non-trivial implications for the owners of small firms. For the most part, these do not lie in the prescriptions they provide so much as the questions they raise. In the case of those principles discussed in this chapter, the most important questions for owners would be:

- What will prevent the cost of achieving a strategy ultimately rising to equal its benefits?
- What is the cost structure of the segment of a market they are considering entering and can any advantages from size be counter-balanced by those from scope or from learning?
- What are the characteristics embodied in their products and what are their shadow prices?

9

MARKET STRUCTURE

One of the principal areas within industrial economies is the relationship between the performance of firms and the characteristics of the elements constituting the markets in which they operate. Michael Porter (1980; 1985) has made a significant contribution within the mainstream of this area but has become one of the most influential of writers on strategy by spelling out the strategic implications to companies of these characteristics. This chapter loosely adopts the framework he proposes but focuses its attention on how the characteristics of the elements of markets might impinge on the strategies formulated by small firms.

The elements it will consider will be:

- Barriers to entry.
- Barriers to exit.
- Buyer power.
- Supplier power.
- Competitive behaviour.

BARRIERS TO ENTRY

It is self-evident that, other factors remaining equal, small firms will achieve higher levels of performance from operating in markets that are growing than those in which total demand is stable or contracting. One of the most important factors that will not remain equal between markets is the ease with which they can be entered. If a market can be entered easily the benefits to incumbent firms from an increase in total demand will prove to be short-lived. The bonus to their profits will be eroded by new entrants. Low entry barriers are not an unmitigated blessing for even potential entrants because they make it difficult to predict their own share of demand.

For a market to prove attractive to small firms implies that one common barrier to entry, that afforded by economies of scale, must be absent. Economies of scope, however, may serve either as a barrier to entry or a facilitator to entry. They will be the former if the combinations of products offered by incumbent firms provide advantages which can only be matched by potential entrants if they are able to offer similar combinations. Examples would be the delivery service offered by a fast-food restaurant, credit facilities provided by used car firms or consultancy on garden design by a horticulturist. These are combinations of different products though used in conjunction with each other. Sometimes the necessity is to produce a broad range of similar products, for instance components or measurement instruments.

On the other hand, economies of scope can ease entry by reducing its cost. The owner of a hotel who turns its basement into a nightclub would be exploiting excess capacity in its space and his previous knowledge of the provision of food and drink. As a result, his costs will be lower than if he were opening a nightclub from scratch.

The barrier to entry which small firms most commonly are able to exploit is the expertise needed to operate in their markets. This would obviously go a long way in explaining why the professions are not, on the whole, over-populated. Moreover, the members of the legal and medical professions have shared with traditional craftsmen an innate understanding of the value to their remuneration of unnecessarily arduous apprenticeships, making it even more difficult to join their ranks. The section on pricing emphasized the need to embody in products characteristics which could not be easily supplied by competitors. The difficulty in doing so would be the barrier around the relevant segment of a market and one major source of such difficulty would be the expertise necessary to create those characteristics. This would clearly be the case with respect to manufactured goods where a change in design is required. But it is hardly coincidence that, across sectors, it is far more likely to be the up-market, high quality segments that are underpopulated, because of the skills needed to operate successfully in these segments.

Barriers to entry can take a variety of forms. An important issue for companies on either side of the barrier, incumbents and potential entrants alike, is how high is it, i.e. how easily can it be overcome. Economists tend to translate height into the expenditure involved, how much it would cost to purchase the necessary capital equipment, for instance, or to recruit managers with the appropriate expertise.

Some barriers cannot so easily be reduced to a question of money. Customer loyalty may not readily be bought through a marketing campaign and this is especially true of the loyalty sometimes accorded to small firms. It is not easy to buy into the networks of small firms supplying the major chains of clothing retailers or manufacturers in the automotive and aerospace sectors. This is because the strength of the networks not only reflects the energy displayed by the salespeople of the supplying firms but the reduction in uncertainty about the quality – or, more accurately, the consistency – of the products supplied. Hence, the barrier to entry is a history of reliability. A similar catch-22, that the failure to display a successful track record acts as a constraint on one ever being achieved, may operate in the markets for financial and legal services, in some sectors exacerbated by prejudices within the professions about what kind of family backgrounds are regarded as most suitable.

The literature on the implications of barriers to entry is vast and here the discussion will not even begin to skim the surface of what is quite a complex topic. One would expect such barriers to lower the volume of competition and that, if the incumbents were sensible, they would avoid a price war that eroded the resulting benefits. Collusion can be overt but usually open discussion is quite unnecessary. Visitors to Manchester's Chinatown will observe a fair amount of consistency in the prices charged, as potential customers may in other areas in which particular trades or professions are geographically concentrated. This could serve as an indication that competition has forced prices down to a level that will only provide a minimum volume of profits but it is more likely that for instance restaurateurs and tailors alike have tacitly recognized that their joint long-term interest lies in higher price levels. In these cases the prices of competitors can be readily monitored and the agreement, which it must be emphasized, need never be explicitly discussed, can be easily policed, deterring mavericks from succumbing to the temptation to break the agreement. The phenomenon is, however, quite likely to be prevalent in sectors in which policing is not quite so straightforward, amongst consultant doctors in private service, for instance, or plumbers. Perhaps the process by which groups of people are able to agree on what is in their joint long-term interest and keep to their agreement in spite of gains to individuals from breaking it is better studied by social anthropologists than economists.[1]

If companies collude on prices, in effect behaving as if they were monopolies or, indeed if they are in the fortunate (for them, not for their customers) position of being sole suppliers, the extent that this will be exploitable through higher prices will depend upon the height of barriers to entry and the elasticity of demand for their products. The former will reflect the ease with which new competitors can enter their markets or, more likely, segment of the market, the latter the readiness of consumers to leave as prices rise.

A straightforward example would be the village shop which possesses a local monopoly in groceries but the prices for which will be constrained by the ability of potential competitors, perhaps the post office or newsagent, to supply groceries and by the willingness of consumers to drive to another shop. If the incursion of new competition required a move of another shop owner into the district or if the population were mostly car-less, the potential for charging higher prices would be correspondingly higher.

Most businesses will draw their customers from particular geographical areas but it would be more useful to define their segments in terms of the characteristics of their products. If products are depicted on a multi-dimensional matrix, each dimension of which represents the amount or presence of a characteristic, whether real or a matter of opinion, the segments would consist in products located together in this matrix and the effects of barriers around the clusters can be analysed in a similar manner to the example of the village store. This abstract concept can be made more concrete with the example of pubs in a town centre offering disco music. They occupy the same segment of the pub market and have the potential to add to the price of their beer. The extent that they are able to do so will depend upon how much they compete amongst themselves on price and, if they collude on price, the extent that customers value the addition of disco music, rather than taking their patronage to other types of pubs, and the ease with which other pubs could offer such music.

BARRIERS TO EXIT

If the economic world were perfectly competitive, firms, which would all be small, would move effortlessly into markets in which above minimum profits were being earned and, equally effortlessly, move out of markets in which they were suffering losses. Most attention, quite rightly, has been devoted to the implications of barriers to entry.

The consequences of barriers to exit have not, however, escaped consideration.

Such barriers can take a number of forms, each of which will have different implications:

- The most obvious would be a lack of alternative activities – a loose term encompassing products produced and the markets in which they are offered – so that firms, for better or worse, are locked into a market. A result of the limited portfolio of management skills embodied in small firms, referred to in Chapter 2, is that those that are in the portfolio may be very activity specific. The same may be said of any other resources employed, most notably capital equipment.

Lack of alternative may be an accurate representation of an owner's plight, or it may be a matter of perception. The distinction is not just semantic. Management courses, creativity seminars, talks with friends and advisers, can all change perceptions about what is possible.

If this change does not occur, or if there really is little else that an owner can do with the resources at his disposal, he will run the distinct risk of being trapped into a market the size of which is incapable of supporting the existing number of competitors. As stated elsewhere, failures will result. Even the eventual survivors will face a painful period during which the shakeout is occurring.

- Owners may be aware that their markets are overcrowded, accept the likelihood of a shakeout, possess the potential of earning an adequate return elsewhere, and yet do not make a timely move because they do not believe that they will be the victims of the shakeout. This belief may be based on a realistic appraisal of their strengths and weaknesses in comparison to that of their competitors or it may be self-deception based on pride. Clearly all firms in an overcrowded market cannot fall into the former category.

The result will be that there will be more firms in a market than would be predicted on the basis of economic rationality, and may be an explanation for the over-capacity in the world automotive sector, and the British newspaper industry. It would not take similar imagination to envisage similar pride among taxi drivers, restaurateurs, private school headmasters and ministers of religion.

Whether this type of barrier ultimately proves fateful depends upon whether competitors leave it too late to recognize that their losses will never be reversed. A difference between small businesses owned by large firms and independent small firms is that the losses incurred by the former may be allowed by their parent company to persist indefinitely, whereas owners of small firms may not find their bank managers quite so sympathetic.

- Though owners may be aware of the alternatives open to them, they may be ignorant of how the returns from them would compare with what they are earning in their current activities and, therefore, do not make a switch because they are not aware that it is in their interests to do so. They certainly may lack even the most rudimentary market intelligence about potential returns from alternatives. The same would not be uncommon among large firms with the resources to collect information on the benefits from producing different products or from selling in new markets.

Owners may also be mistaken in their assessment of the returns from their current activities, especially if producing a range of products. Again even large firms are often inaccurate in their estimation of costs, especially of their use of capital equipment and of land, and in their allocation of costs between products. One can hardly expect small firms to display greater efficiency in this regard.

COMPETITIVE BEHAVIOUR

The size distribution of firms will vary dramatically between sectors. Of crucial importance to small firms is whether these distributions make any difference to their performance. If there are significant economies of scale the answer will be strongly in the affirmative. In the long-term small firms could not expect to compete with much bigger firms head-on and survive.

There are several reasons why co-existence between firms of different sizes may occur:

- The benefits from size have not yet been realized. This situation would be most likely in new markets, which have attracted firms of varying sizes, and in which it is not evident whether size of firm makes very much difference to success. An example might be business systems software.
- Large firms may have opted, in a manner ingenuously analysed by Scherer (1980), to exploit the potential threat to new entrants from economies of scale by charging high prices rather than by expanding production to the minimum efficient scale, at which lowest

costs could be achieved. The threat of expansion, and the resulting price war, might be sufficient to deter entry from other large firms or the benefits to incumbents may be short-term, but in either case, small firms could shelter under the price umbrella because it would not be in the interests of the dominant firms to cut their prices to drive them out.

- There may not be any advantages from size. This is certainly a theoretical possibility but examples are difficult to find. Empirically size is not correlated with profitability among quoted companies but there is a big difference between economies at the level of a quoted company, which are usually collections of businesses, and the economies associated with expanding each of these businesses. Firms can become too big or complex to manage efficiently but this does not imply their constituent businesses are too big.
- The most common reason for the peaceful co-existence of large and small firms within the same market is that they occupy different segments, even different niches within segments. It may be that small firms operate at the quality end of the market, or perhaps focus on the needs of particular types of consumers or perhaps produce specialist products without any particular types of customer in mind.

RELATIONSHIP WITH BUYERS AND SELLERS

A small firm will form part of a chain consisting, at one end, of basic inputs and, at the other, of the final consumer. Its management of the relationship with customers and suppliers may prove of crucial importance to its level of performance, even survival. This section will discuss relations with customers in terms of:

- Relative power.
- Wider perspective than power-relationships.
- The implications of lean manufacturing.

and will conclude with a consideration of one type of relationship with suppliers, franchising.

BUYER POWER

Some categories of small firms, usually those supplying services, will sell direct to the final consumer. Examples would be retailers, restaurateurs, taxi drivers and hairdressers. Manufacturers may sell direct if they market through mail order or if they are vertically integrated into retailing, a not uncommon feature in some segments of the baking, confectionery and clothing sectors. Otherwise a small firm must conduct its business by either selling intermediate goods to another manufacturer, or finished goods to a retailer.

It should be emphasized that a small firm's customers may themselves be small and that relative power within their relationship will depend upon the sort of factors listed below. Indeed, these factors will also determine its negotiating position *vis-à-vis* its suppliers. It is perfectly possible for a small firm to be in a position to exploit buyer power, irrespective of the degree to which it is itself a victim.

However, quite rightly, buyer power is usually discussed in the context of the relationship of small to large companies. This is certainly the case in a comprehensive international review carried out on behalf of the Organization for Economic Co-operation and Development (OECD, 1981). Its definition of buyer power is as good as might be found anywhere else:

> The situation which exists when a firm or group of firms, either because it has a dominant position as a purchaser of a product or a service or because it has strategic or leverage advantages as a result of its size or other characteristics, is able to obtain from a supplier more favourable terms than those available to other buyers. The degree of a firm's buying power is closely dependent on the magnitude of the costs or other disadvantage which it can occasion to its suppliers by ceasing to buy from them and, conversely, on the extra costs and other disadvantages which it can itself incur in the consequence of the change of supplier.

The tone of the report, which is largely concerned with the relationship of suppliers to retailers, does not suggest the degree of converse power to be very great. Felgner (1989) would lend support to this pessimism. Though he draws on American experience it would be equally pertinent in the European context. Among other reasons, he ascribes the increase in the relative power of retailers to:

- The sheer volume of their purchases.
- The high degree of buyer concentration.
- The rapid expansion of major retailing chains during the 1970s and 1980s.
- The superior knowledge about the relative profitability of pro-

ducts, especially as it affects the allocation of shelf space, that is afforded by computer scanning.

- The maturity of some products weakening suppliers' negotiating position.

Cunningham (1993), explores, in some depth, the basis of the power possessed by buyers and sellers in an industrial context, though many of his points would be relevant to supplier–retailer relationships.

Cunningham reminds the reader that buyers can enjoy the fruits of their power in ways other than in the price that they pay, for instance:

- In the commercial and technical information with which they are provided.
- The size of stockholdings that their suppliers are forced to carry.
- Delivery times.

To this might be added a high position in the queue if supplies must be rationed, for any reason, between customers and, more important, easy credit terms. Indeed, one of the most commonly expressed complaints within the small firm community is the difficulty it faces when attempting to achieve prompt payment from large customers.

The list of sources of buyer-power that Cunningham presents is formidably long, though it includes factors which, whilst certainly strengthening a customer's negotiating position, would not normally be described as power-enhancing, for instance the quality of the information that the supplier is able to receive from a buyer, and the willingness of the latter to accommodate its supplier's preferences regarding product specification, stockholding and commercial terms. If anything, the last might be construed as a measure of the power of the supplier rather than the source of the power of the buyer.

Factors which could be described as a priori likely to increase the power of customers would include:

- The buyer purchases a high proportion of the supplier's total output.
- The customer can readily find alternative supplies.
- The customer is currently supplied from multiple sources.
- The product is easy to design or manufacture, perhaps by the customer itself.
- The requirements for the product can be easily specified, removing the need for extensive product tests.
- The supplier has had to make special adaptations to the product to

101

suit the customer, with the result that it may not be easy to sell elsewhere.

- The relationship between the buyer and seller has only been established a short time, so that customer-specific products have not yet been supplied (though this approaches being a contradiction of the previous point).

Suppliers, however, are not without sources of power, including:

- The product cannot be purchased from an alternative source.
- It would prove difficult to design and manufacture the product from scratch.
- Extensive testing would be needed before products from an alternative source could be used.
- The customer has had to make adjustments to meet the needs of suppliers.

Clearly these are virtually mirror images of the sources of buyer power and, again, some of the alleged sources of supplier power might be interpreted, in fact, as symptoms of quite the reverse, of the weakness of suppliers *vis-à-vis* their customers, for instance if they sell at a low price. Even the 'loyalty' displayed by customers may be interpreted as evidence of their being perfectly satisfied with the deal they have extracted from their suppliers, rather than of the power of the latter.

What is pertinent to the purposes of this book is the extent that small firms are able to exercise any countervailing power to that of their larger customers. If they possess a monopoly in the supply of a useful product without any readily available substitutes they may well possess real power but examples among small firms are rare and would be most likely to occur with businesses based on a high level of specialist knowledge, in high technology, perhaps, or the up-market segments of the professions, supplying to non-retailing firms. It is uncommon for small firms whose customers are the retailing chains to possess significant countervailing power because the value of their products would only form a very small proportion of the total revenue earned by the chains.

THE WIDER PERSPECTIVE

Small firms are not likely to possess very much power in their dealings with large firms in the sense that they can exercise coercion. They may well, however, possess power in conforming to the wider definition presented by Cunningham (op. cit.):

> All resources that a party can exploit in order to effect the behaviour of the other ... Any circumstances or condition of the relationship which makes one party dependent on the other, forms a basis of power.

It would not be unusual for a small firm to possess a high degree of what Cunningham calls 'referent' power, an example of which would be that 'the customer has learnt to know the supplier well, habits and procedures have become established, and the relationship is partly maintained on the basis of convenience and inertia'.

The implication would be that the customer is content with the relationship, that it suits him. Moreover, though a risk that is run when changing to a new supplier is that it will prove, in some way, to be unreliable, and this may serve, as Cunningham (op. cit.) correctly argues, as a further force binding customer to an established supplier, its effect is surely not to generate quite the same degree of resentment within customers as when they perceive that they face little alternative to purchasing from a particular supplier. A track record of reliability hardly provides a company with sufficient muscle to charge monopoly prices.

The recognition that there are various types of relationships between industrial customers and suppliers, and that these can be very complex, prompted the initiation of the influential International Marketing and Purchasing Group (IMP) Project [2] which has led to a large number of important publications.[3] The approach of the IMP group is perhaps best summed up by Ford (1980):

> The Interaction Approach ... sees buyer–seller relationships taking place between two active parties. This is in contrast to the more traditional view of marketing which analyses the reaction of an aggregate market to a seller's offering. The interaction approach considers that either buyer or seller may take the initiative in seeking a partner. Further, both companies are likely to be involved in adaptions to their own process or product technologies to accommodate each other. Neither party is likely to be able to make unilateral changes in its activities as buyer or seller without consultation, or at least consideration, of their individual opposite numbers.

Campbell (1985) considers in detail the circumstances that will lead to particular types of relationships which he categorizes into:

- Independent, conducted rather at arm's length through the market mechanism.
- Dependent, in which one party is in a dominant position.
- Interdependent, where buyers and sellers are 'both willing to establish a long-term relationship, to exchange information openly and to trust each other'.

The appropriate strategies for suppliers will vary with the nature of the relationship. For those supplying within an independent relationship, Campbell argues:

> A careful balance has to be struck between the advantages of differentiating the product by providing additional services and the disadvantages of a price which is out of step with the market price.

For the firm subject to 'command' purchasing the 'supplier's role is to do the buyer's bidding, and the keys to success are flexibility, personal attention to the buying company's needs, and efficient production facilities'.

The advice is most fulsome regarding the appropriate strategy for managing a co-operative relationship. Customers must be provided, for instance, with reassurance that they had made the right decision so 'Senior management ... must visit these customers and take every opportunity to develop social changes', and suppliers are warned against the temptation of exploiting customer loyalty through higher prices.

The most comprehensive attempt to test the IMP model has been made by Metcalf, Frear and Krishnan (1992), using data from the American aero-engine industry. They consider the influences on the degree of co-operation between producers and their suppliers, defined as the degree of 'adaptation', 'the extent to which the buyer and seller make substantial investments in the relationship'.

Co-operation is to some extent related to the amount of social and information exchange that takes place. The former was measured by responses to such statements as 'Buyer/seller has a good understanding of our problems as buyers/sellers'.

Information exchange refers to the amount of technical documentation that was provided. The level of explanatory power of the model, though, is not particularly high.

Rather more success is achieved in predicting the degree of adaptation, which was related to the extent of co-operation and information exchange between companies and on a product's perceived importance to the customer, measured both in terms of how crucial the component was to the functioning of the engine and of the value attached to the characteristics of the components, such as their reliability.

LEAN PRODUCTION

The best example of a relationship between customer and supplier based on co-ordination is that depicted by Womack, Jones and Roos (1990) in their influential description of the Japanese auto-industry. The theme of their book is a comparison between mass production, as once epitomized by General Motors, and the 'lean production' invented by Toyota. The latter is not clearly defined anywhere but is presented as a comprehensive series of examples of how Japanese companies are apparently able to both achieve higher quality and to operate a Just-in-Time system of production, requiring very low levels of stocks. For the most part the reader is confronted with a catalogue of methods by which the Japanese are able to be more efficient than their competitors.

The implications of lean production for the suppliers to Japanese auto-producers are quite far reaching. Consider, first, the quintessential ways in which the relationship to their suppliers is managed by mass producers:

- They are provided with a specification for a component or part of a component. It will include the design of the product; the minimum level of quality, which translates into the maximum incidence of defects that will be tolerated; and maximum delivery times.

The contract will then be awarded on the basis of price with stiff penalties if any of the terms of the agreement are broken.

- The relationship is essentially adversarial, based on the assumption that supplier and customer can gain only at the other's expense. At best the mass producer will be indifferent to the profits earned by its suppliers, at worst would view a high level as evidence that it had failed to gain the maximum advantage from its negotiations. Mutual distrust would be confirmed by short contract lengths. Each party would divulge as little information as possible, in particular suppliers would not dream of providing details of their costs. Moreover, in their arms length relationship with their customers there would be no incentive to divulge any more than is absolutely necessary, nor to provide any comments or advice on what they are being asked to supply. Nor would there be any reason for them to exchange information with other suppliers, certainly not of the same products, indeed, absolutely the reverse, but even of other products. Unfortunately, given the inter-connections between components, this could have damaging consequences in terms of the quality of the final products.

Womack, Jones and Roos (op. cit.) are laudatory in their praise of Japanese methods and, if they are right in their assessment, the contrast could not be more extreme:

- The philosophy behind the relationship between buyers and suppliers is that they are working together for their mutual benefit and is not characterized by the mutual mistrust that is likely to be present between even in-house suppliers in mass producers and their customers, the assemblers. One result is that manufacturers decide first on the price of the car and work backwards to establish how it can be made to provide a reasonable return for both buying and supplying companies. The latter are chosen on their track records and emphatically not on the basis of price.

- Suppliers work with their customers on the design of components, perhaps seconding resident design engineers to them. This is assisted by responsibility for whole components, for instance a seat, being delegated to particular suppliers, who may then subcontract individual parts to other specialist companies. One result is that, whereas the mass producers will be supplied by 1,000–2,500 companies, if its own subsidiaries are included, the lean producer will manage with less than 300, or rather, will need to manage less than 300 separate relationships.

- Information is readily exchanged between customers and suppliers and directly between suppliers. The latter process is facilitated by supplier associations which have been important for disseminating new ideas, from total quality control in the late 1950s, through value engineering in the 1960s, to computer aided design in the 1980s. As the authors point out, as it would be unthinkable for suppliers of mass producers to provide information that could undermine their own competitive position, the role of supplier associations in the West would be taken by professional associations, though, they would argue, not very effectively.

- Lean production requires that deliveries be made directly to the assembly line, with no inspection. The lack of safety nets implied by stocks and inspection means that mistakes might prove catastrophic.

When a mistake does occur the supplier will not necessarily be dismissed, as it might expect from a mass producer. Instead as a penalty it will lose a fraction of its business to an alternative supplier for a fixed period of time. The emphasis is, however, on establishing the reason for any mistakes and Toyota apparently achieves this by asking a succession of 'five whys'. The example given by Womack *et al.* (op. cit.) is of remorseless thoroughness:

First they discover that the defective part has been caused by a machine that cannot hold a proper tolerance. But the machine isn't the ultimate cause. So the team asks: 'Why can't this machine hold tolerance?' The supplier's personnel report that it is because the machine operators cannot be adequately trained. The team members ask 'Why?' The supplier answers that it's because these employees keep quitting to look for other work which means the operators are always novices. 'Why do workers keep quitting?'. 'Because the work is monotonous... '. The ultimate resolution: to rethink the work process in order to reduce turnover. This at last is the ultimate cause.

As Womack *et al.* point out pure mass production in its pure form no longer exists, with Western producers of cars adopting, to varying degrees, at least some of the elements of lean production. Clearly, this will have ramifications for their UK suppliers of components, and, of course, suppliers to UK-based Japanese car companies are already gaining an understanding of the implications to them of lean production. Carr and Truesdale (1992) paint a detailed picture of the approach adopted by Nissan's supplier-selection team in their search, not for the component that would be best in its class, as would their opposite numbers in Ford or Rover, but for a long-term relationship with a supplier that would prove the best. This search involves visiting factories and:

Following products from design and development through the full manufacturing process. At all stages they look for planning, tidiness, appearance of the shop, how busy the workers are, how many machines are running and professionalism... Management attitude, technical capability and delivery reliability are considered much more important than a supplier's location or its size or marketing/publicity material.

(Carr and Truesdale, 1992)

Some suppliers may well regard lean production as a somewhat mixed blessing.

The significance of lean production to small firms is wider in that those operating in one sector are having to change their attitudes to their customers. The evidence from the IMP and subsequent studies is of increasing variety in the nature of buyer–supplier relationships, of more major companies acknowledging that the traditional 'arm's length' and adversarial relationship with their suppliers may not be in their best interest. Even some of the big retail chains, hardly arm's length in their dealings with suppliers, but with a reputation for squeezing the most advantage from their dominant position, are apparently beginning to modify their attitudes.

FRANCHISING

Completing the picture requires a discussion of the relationship of small firms to their suppliers. The broad principles differ little from those governing the buyer–seller relationships as discussed in the last sections. Small firms may possess a degree of power in their relationship to their suppliers and may choose to exploit this power or, irrespective of their potential to do so, may prefer a co-operative relationship, which would certainly be encouraged if their own customers had adopted strategies involving co-operation.

The more likely scenario, however, would be that a small firm will be in a comparatively weak position in its relationship with suppliers. It may be forced to pay, quite literally, a penalty for its lack of size, either from being a victim of market-power or because of its inability to bulk purchase. It may also suffer in other ways, being pushed to the end of the queue for deliveries, for instance, or in the terms of credit it is offered.

Small firms are almost certainly the victims of the power of banks, their major suppliers of external capital. This section will limit its attention however, to a particular type of relationship,[4] franchising, that a small firm might have with its suppliers. In this the franchisee sells the product, system or process of the franchisor (Johns et al.,

1989). Examples of products would be Tupperware utensils and Avon cosmetics, of systems would be fast foods, such as Burger King, and car rentals, such as Hertz, and of processes would be where essential ingredients are provided to the manufacturer, for example, by Coca Cola.

Franchising covers a surprisingly broad spectrum of activities and is growing in importance. According to the British Franchise Association in 1995 there were 220 franchisers and McCosker (1988) has estimated over seven million to be employed in the US franchised sector.

Franchising usually possesses the following features:

- Franchisees are provided with ready-made businesses, usually a local monopoly of an established trade name, which may be nationally advertised. The franchisor will provide its know-how and the muscle to bulk buy. The franchisee will provide the capital, though often the franchisor will have negotiated with a bank to secure this on favourable terms. As franchisees will only have been selected after an initial, sometimes quite intensive, screening they will represent a safer bet to a bank than the average potential small business.
- Profits from individual businesses will be shared by both parties and, though agreements will vary in how the spoils are divided, in all cases, franchisees can expect to gain in remuneration from the success of their businesses. They are, in that sense, independent businesses.
- Initiative may be severely restricted, however. Franchisors may allow very little scope for their franchisees to exhibit any innovation in what or how they sell. A fast food chain, for instance, may lay down strict guidelines not only on matters such as price, decor, cleanliness or recipes, but even on the precise form of address to be made by sales staff to customers. Regular inspection can be expected to assure compliance. If, in spite of these constraints, a franchisee is able to prove particularly successful, she may face the risk of her business being repurchased by the franchisor at a pre-determined price, as some franchising agreements provide just such a provision. Moreover, some agreements, though certainly not all, limit franchisees to one outlet, regardless of their success.

Franchising may be depicted as offering the opportunity to run one's own business, but, in practice, where conditions are tight, there is very little difference from working for a company operating a system of payment by results. Such a system would be introduced as a motivational tool and the modern view of franchising (as suggested, for instance, by McMahon *et al.*, 1993) is that it should be put in the context of problems faced by each group of stakeholders in an organization in policing the behaviour of those controlling it, where 'stakeholders' are all those whose interests are in any way affected by the organization. The fashionable label for the power struggle between stakeholders is 'principal agent problem', the agents being those stakeholders in control of an organization, on behalf of the others, designated the principals.

The study of some aspects of such struggles has a long history in the managerial theories of the firm (Marris, 1964; Williamson, 1964), in which attention is focused on the difficulties confronted by shareholders in quoted companies in ensuring that their management pursue policies that are consistent with profit maximization rather than, say, empire building, excessive growth, executive perks or a quiet life. This tradition does not employ the terms, principals and agencies, which are usually credited to Jensen and Meckling (1976).

It would be unfair to dismiss the principal agent issue as merely a new name for the managerial theories of the firm because the conflicts the former encompasses are set in a wider context than simply that between owners and managers. In small firms, some owners may act as chief executives and, therefore, would not face any problems in controlling the actions of their workforce, including managers, but they, themselves, could be represented as the agents of non-executive co-owners, who could be depicted as their principals. Moreover, the financial management of small firms can also be viewed in a principal agent framework (Hand, Lloyd and Rogow, 1982). External suppliers of finance, most notably banks, must initially evaluate the riskiness of a business, when its owners have a vested interest in portraying this at a minimum level and, subsequently, suppliers of capital must monitor how the capital they have provided is being spent, in spite of possible efforts by owners at directing it to ends not originally agreed at the time it was provided.

Some evidence for the importance now attached to principal agency by writers on small firm financial management is provided by Patrick Hutchinson (1991) who waxes lyrical on its significance:

Agency theory helps to explain why small firms exist at all. Given the existence of economies of size, it could be expected that all business activities would be conducted by large organi-

110

zations. Agency theory provides counter-balancing arguments in favour of smallness. In some cases the disbenefits of size are not sufficient to outweigh the benefits of economics of size and in these cases large firms will predominate. In other cases, where economies of size are not great or where agency costs are very great, small size may be the optimum.

Franchising would represent an attempt by firms to gain the benefits from size without incurring the costs of ensuring that employees carry out their work most effectively. Such costs will be particularly high in activities characterized by multiple plants or outlets. In even the best run empires it can prove difficult to control what is happening in far-flung outposts.

If franchising is regarded as a solution to the problems of managing a big company it may be helpful to our understanding of the small-firm sector to regard, in the same light, other forms of relationship between big and small companies, and this would certainly be the implication of the point by Hutchinson quoted above. When Coase (1937) asked the question of what constitutes a firm he answered in terms of the circumstances under which it would be optimal to own resources rather than rely on its provision in the market place, in other words, the classic make or buy decision.

Whether a firm is able or willing to adopt a command relationship with its suppliers or prefers one of co-operation it has adopted either option in preference to vertically integrating backwards and carrying out the activity in-house. Principal agent theory would provide a ready explanation of why it should have made this decision. If a franchisee is only a private company in a very limited sense and might be regarded, for all intents and purposes, as an adjunct of its franchisor, much the same might be said of a supplier locked into a tight relationship with a dominant customer. This would throw into sharp perspective the notion that the advantages to owners of running a small firm lie in their sense of independence, or even in the scope for displaying creativity. They might just as well be running one of their customer's subsidiaries.

CONCLUDING REMARKS

The structure and characteristics of its markets will influence the performance of a small firm though whether the strength of that influence will prove stronger than internal factors, specifically how it is managed, can only be established empirically, the subject of Chapters 11 and 12.

The height of barriers to entry will certainly serve as an important factor in determining both a small firm's choice of market and the volume, if not degree, of competition that it will face. Barriers to exit may affect detrimentally the levels of performance it achieves. The size of competitors may matter but if a small firm is a victim of the advantages provided by scale, this raises some interesting questions about why the situation has arisen.

Small firms may suffer at the hands of more powerful customers, though the practices adopted by Japanese auto-producers serve as evidence that this need not be inevitable.

Franchising represents a special sort of relationship with suppliers. It may well prove attractive to the would-be owner of a small business and may provide a higher income than if she were truly independent but some of the joy from such independence may be denied by the restrictions usually incorporated into a franchising agreement.

10

ORGANIZATION LIFECYCLES

Over time a business will change. Some changes will reflect the need to respond to new threats or opportunities, which can arise in even the most stable of environments, some will reflect a failure to meet a threat – indeed the change in question may be into liquidation – or the change may result from the fruits of success, most obviously the expansion of the business. Other changes can occur, to varying degrees, autonomously of what is happening in the environment. They can affect any aspect of running the company, from the grandest strategies, through to its organizational structure, down to the time of its coffee break.

The issue to be addressed here is whether there is any pattern to the changes, whether it would be valid to think in terms of an organizational lifecycle. Such a term readily conjures up the concept of the product lifecycle which was once popular within marketing but is now largely discredited. In its crudest form this implied a general shape to the distribution of sales over time, consisting of several phases: launch, take-off, maturity, decline. There are parallels, not least that in adopting the language of biology, especially 'lifecycle', but it is also common to speak of the birth, death and maturity of products and companies, it is easy to fall into the trap of imposing a quite spurious framework. There is nothing inevitable about either product or corporate decline – in the language of lifecycles either could prove, for all intents and purposes, 'immortal', and certainly with products, the case with companies will be discussed in a moment, it is possible to stave-off all of the symptoms of 'middle age', so that precious little consistency is demonstrated in the patterns of sales over time. If there is a most common lifecycle for either products or companies it would consist in birth followed shortly afterwards by death.

The literature on organization lifecycles that is of relevance to small firms[1] can be divided into:

- Linkages of stages to owner characteristics.
- Theories relating a broad range of internal factors to the growth of a company.
- Empirical evidence on organization lifecycles.

OWNER CHARACTERISTICS

The literature on this is embedded in the tradition that it is valid to classify owners of small firms into types and raises the question of whether the characteristics associated with the founders of companies will necessarily be the most appropriate for managing subsequent growth. Stanworth and Curran (1976) while explicitly rejecting the notion of inevitability of stages of organizational development do categorize owner-managers into types. The priorities of 'artisans' are personal autonomy and satisfaction from their work and, if anything, they have an aversion to growth, if this requires a change to a more systematic and bureaucratic style of management. As the firms grow the most appropriate characteristics would be those associated with the 'classical entrepreneurs', with their emphasis on the maximization of financial returns, and, subsequently, with 'managers', who would be more professionally orientated than artisans and less prone to feelings of social marginality. They argue that second and third generation owners are more likely to be managerial, by implication a move in emphasis from the effects of growth on owner-characteristics to the effects of time. In a more recent work Curran has put more stress on the importance of situational factors, such as state of demand (Curran and Blackburn, 1994).

For Smith and Miner (1983) the contrast is between 'craftsmen entrepreneurs', with their narrow education, feelings of social inadequacy and limited time-horizons, and 'opportunitistic entrepreneurs', who are the opposite. They argue that the former would face great difficulties in managing the growth of their companies, the latter much less so. Smith and Miner use psychological tests to compare the characteristics of founders of small firms with those of managers of variously sized companies. They conclude:

> Entrepreneurs are not like top level corporate managers or even middle-level managers. They are less favourably inclined towards authority figures, less competitive (particularly in games)

and less assertive than managers in large business organizations. It would appear likely, as many have hypothesised, that a size-able percentage of entrepreneurs would have difficulty heading up a growing organization as it moved to a size where a bureau-cratic system was needed.

Similar comments might be made on this type of research as were made in Chapter 6.

STAGES AND GROWTH

Although product lifecycle models attempt to predict the pattern of sales over time, organization lifecycle models are usually concerned with internal changes that will occur as the firm grows in size. Whereas Greiner (1972) may claim age to be: 'the most obvious and essential dimension for any model of development' (of the stages of an organ-ization) his well-known model is really about changes in responses to growth. Most of the crisis he so eloquently describes would not have occurred if the company had maintained stable sales and had simply grown older. This would be the implication of Churchill and Lewis (1983) who, when describing the pitfalls from growing, emphasize that these can be avoided if owners choose to remain stable yet profitable.

In his review of the literature Kazanjian (1988) listed a plethora of three, four and five plus stage models. Fairly typical would be Chur-chill and Lewis (1983) in which there are five possible stages:

1 *Existence* in which, 'The company's strategy is simply to remain alive'; 'The owner *is* the business, performs all the important tasks, and is the major supplier of energy, direction; and, with relatives and friends, capital'.
2 *Survival* where the emphasis shifts from mere existence to break-ing even in the short-term and, in the longer term, financing growth. This stage is characterized by: lack of formality and systems; the dominance of the owners over all aspects of the business. Firms may continue in this stage for long periods, earning only marginal returns, eventually ceasing to trade with the retire-ment of the owners.
3 *Success* At this stage the owners face a choice between: 'whether to exploit the company's accomplishments and expand or keep the company stable and profitable, providing a base for alternative owner activities'. If the company chooses the latter, the 'Success–

115

Disengagement sub-stage', it can indefinitely earn a healthy return provided 'environmental change does not destroy its market niche or ineffective management reduce its competitive abilities'. The company would be characterized by: recruitment of functional and line managers; delegation of some management responsibilities; owner's strategy is essentially to maintain status quo; over time, the owner moves apart from the company, reflecting his outside interests and the increasing importance in decision-making of his managers. Alternatively, the owner may choose to capitalize on his success to aim for the 'Success–Growth sub-stage'. This would be associated with: strategic planning by the owners; more systemized decision-making; greater risk, than in previous stages, of cashflow problems.

4 *Take-off* having achieved a launch into growth the owners will be forced to face the problems that their success will bring, especially those associated with the degree of delegation they will contemplate and with the generation of sufficient cash to finance their company's expansion. This is the 'pivotal' stage in which the company can become established or, if not, it can be sold at a profit. This is the point at which the limitation of the founders become most acute. Successful management of this stage will usually imply: significant delegation by the owner; divisionalization; operational and strategic planning; possibly replacement of the founder, either voluntarily, or involuntarily, by the company's investors or creditors.

5 *Resource Maturity* the company 'has now arrived. It has the advantages of size, financial resources and managerial talent'. It is characterized by: formal management tools, such as 'budgets, strategic planning, management by objectives and standard cost systems'; separation of the owner from his business 'both financially and operationally'; the danger of 'ossification', defined as a 'lack of innovative decision-making and avoidance of risks'.

It must be emphasized that in the Churchill and Lewis model the stages presented are certainly not inevitable. Firms may fail to move to a successive stage or, especially in the third, may choose not to.

Greiner (*op. cit.*), in his influential paper, distinguishes between 'evolutionary' and 'revolutionary' periods. During the former 'only modest adjustments appear necessary for maintaining growth under the same overall pattern of management'. Whereas revolutionary periods display 'serious upheaval' in management practices. An interesting feature of Greiner's model is that 'each phase is both an effect of the previous phase and a cause for the next phase'.

The phases are:

- *Creativity* in which: founders concentrate on making and selling and disdain management activities; internal communication is frequent and informal; marketing is reactive to customer needs; hours of work are long and rewards modest.

But the previous management style and corporate culture which facilitated the creativity of the initial phase become increasingly inappropriate for managing the fruits of its success. A strong business manager is required to manage the growing company. The crisis can be resolved if the founders recognize their inadequacies and allow a professional administrator to take responsibility for introducing tight organization.

- *Direction* in which: a functional organization is introduced; information becomes more systemized; communication becomes more formal; power shifts from the lower level supervisors to the new management team.

The crisis during this phase results from the lack of opportunity offered by the rigid hierarchy to lower level managers to exploit their superior knowledge of pertinent aspects of the company. The key issue is then whether senior management is prepared to move towards a greater degree of delegation.

- *Delegation* in which: the organization is divided into profit centres; headquarters staff manage by exception, based on periodic reports.

The crisis during this phase arises from the increased power of the managers of the profit centres. These barons become more interested in running their own fiefdoms than being concerned with the interests of the organization as a whole. The size and complexity of the organization (Greiner might well have added the effects of reactionary political in-fighting) act as a deterrent to a return to centralized management. As an alternative, some sort of co-ordination process is required.

- *Co-ordination* This comprises the use of formal systems to achieve what Greiner describes as greater co-ordination, though it would be legitimate to question whether this is, in fact, little different from a return to the centralized management structure which he argues would be difficult. Regardless of the label attached to this phase, its features are: increased formalization of planning procedures; merger of decentralized units into product groups; these product groups are treated as 'investment centres' between which capital is allocated on the basis of profitability. (It is not clear on what criteria funds were distributed between the previous profit centres); increase in number of head office staff, to 'initiate company-wide programmes of control and review for line managers'. Not surprisingly, given the thrust of Greiner's thesis, this increase in bureaucratization leads to a 'red tape crisis' in which 'procedures take precedence over problem solving' and friction is exacerbated between line and staff management, and between headquarters and the field. The issue is now whether it is possible for bureaucrats to introduce a more flexible system.

- *Collaboration* If this phase is achieved the emphasis is upon 'a more flexible and behavioural approach to management'. This translates into, among other features: much more team work, both inter-disciplinary and combining headquarters and field staff; reduction in the number of head office staff; introduction of matrix-type structures; less formalization in systems; encouragement of experiments in new practices.

At the time of writing his paper, Greiner, 1972, was only able to conjecture as to the crisis that would beset companies in the as yet final phase though, given the time that has elapsed since, there is clearly some scope for his theory to be updated.

What is not at all clear from Greiner's analysis is the consequences of failing to survive each successive crisis. If 'evolution is not an automatic affair, it is a contest for survival' is taken literally there would appear to be a certain inevitability about the stages of development in Greiner's model.

ORGANIZATIONAL LIFECYCLE MODELS – AN APPRAISAL

Although the models just discussed have been presented, for the sake of completeness, in their entirety, only the early stages are of relevance to the owners of small firms. Yet if there is any strong empirical evidence of organization development it is of a move to greater divisionalization by larger firms. Following Chandler (1962), Wil-

liamson (1970) and Channon (1973) there are good reasons for expect-
ing firms with a range of major activities to divisionalize into profit
centres, if for no other reason than that this facilitates the introduction
of a simple method of monitoring their performance. It is in the
interests of the senior managers within profit centres to empire-build
and generally pursue policies that are in their parochial interests.
Relative profitability provides a more straightforward criteria for
appraisal, and therefore serves as a better antidote to such empire
building, than might be applied to the functional areas that were
replaced by the profit centres. There are no obvious ways of assessing
the efficiency, for instance, of the finance or marketing departments.

Otherwise the theories of other aspects of the organizational development of large firms are not particularly strong and have even less
force with respect to small. Whereas, self-evidently, firms undergo
changes the most important influence on when these occur, and their
direction, need not be their growth rates. The age of companies, for
instance, or internal politics or factors external but not reflected in
their growth, may all be contributing factors. It may not be completely
without significance, moreover, that the relative importance of the
influences on their failure as perceived by the owners of insolvent
firms (Chapter 4), would appear to vary with a host of factors as well
as the size of the firms. It is not uncommon for theories, on whatever
topic, to generate a set of ideal types, each of which possess specific
characteristics but their proponents would usually concede the pertinence of extraneous factors and would accept that whether the
'noise' from these factors is sufficiently heavy to render their ideal
types unobservable can only be resolved empirically. Perhaps this is
being grossly unfair, but writers who theorize on stages of organization development appear to possess an unusual amount of faith that
their broad generalizations about the combinations of factors that will
be found together in firms experiencing the same stage of development
will actually be reflected in reality.

Lifecycle theories are least convincing with respect to small firms.
The longer they survive the greater the variety of problems with which
they will be buffeted and it may well be that the founders will need to
augment their portfolio of management talent, as suggested in Chapter
2, or to introduce any of many other kinds of changes, but the
transition from being a small- to a medium-sized company, although
involving a large percentage increase in the volume of sales, need not
produce the traumas assumed in the lifecycle literature. Much will
hinge on whether founders intrinsically possess personal charac-

teristics which will prove inappropriate for the management of their firm if it succeeds in growing. As might be inferred from Chapter 6, a certain degree of scepticism may be warranted about the legitimacy of stereotyping the founders of small firms.

The most well known empirical study of organization lifecycles has been undertaken by Miller and Friesen, who have published their results in a number of articles, the most pertinent, of which for the purposes of this discussion, would be Miller and Friesen (1982).[2] This considered the history, over at least twenty years, of thirty-six companies. As the authors readily concede, their sample is weighted towards large well known companies and excludes those that failed early in their life.

The characteristics of companies were scored on fifty-four factors encompassing their strategies, 'situation' (a mixture of internal and external), structure and decision-making style. When related to the phase of development of the companies their conclusions broadly confirmed the typologies presented above, indeed extending the breadth of the generalization. For instance, firms in the birth phase, among many other attributes, achieve a viable product market strategy: 'by trial and error ... (involving) major and frequent product or service innovations... and the conscious pursuit of a niche strategy.' A result of such niche strategies is that 'markets tend not to be hostile or competitive'.

Their management style is characterized by 'extreme conservatism. There is little innovation ... an abhorrence of risk taking and a reluctance to even imitate competitors' innovations', and the structure is both centralized and lacking in efficient management information systems.

For small firms the pertinent question would be what changes would occur as they entered the growth phase and, again, we are presented with unequivocal profiles.

Growth is achieved through a:

> More complete array of products for a given market rather than positions in widely varying markets. Market segmentation begins to play a role, with managers trying to identify specific sub-groups of customers and to make small product or service modifications in order to better serve them.

The situation of firms in the growth phase is that:

> They are generally bigger than their competitors... Markets

become more heterogeneous than in the birth stage, perhaps in large part because product lines have been broadened. This broadening also results in more direct confrontations with the competition as the niche strategy is abandoned.

The structure becomes departmentalized and manned with functionally based staff and, increasingly, by 'well educated technocrats'.

The decision-making is now less risk-taking and proactive, involving more team decisions which:

Can limit the boldness of decisions as the most daring proposals may be questioned by conservative managers ... It is important to point out, however, that power is still quite centralized and that decisions ... are by no means conservative. Boldness continues to prevail.

The owners of small firms, therefore, can be assured that success will not diminish the boldness they displayed when they founded their companies.

Two reservations might be expressed about Miller and Friesen's methodology. Although full credit must be given to the formidable volume of work that was required to produce thirty-six histories, the sample is simply not sufficiently large to allow the authors to make such sweeping generalizations. Second, their criteria for allocating a period of a company's life to a particular phase consisted not only of objectively measurable growth rates but the characteristics of the companies. Firms in the birth phase had 'informal structures' and were 'dominated by owner manager'; those in the growth phase had 'functionally organized structure, early formalization of policies'; in the maturity phase had 'more bureaucratic organization'. Characteristics of companies included: 'Revival' 'diversification of product lines, divisionalization, use of sophisticated controls and planning systems' and 'Decline' a 'low rate of product innovation'.

Arguably, however, these criteria were some of the hypotheses that should have been tested. It is not obvious, for instance, how a firm would be classified if a revival in its growth had not been accompanied by divisionalization yet such restructuring could have led to many of its other characteristics.[3]

Laying aside these reservations, the straightforwardness of the conclusions that might be drawn from Miller and Friesen's work is a little marred by the lack of predictable sequence to the phases. When the histories of the thirty-six companies are divided into 161 periods, 125 of which are adjacent to each other:

- Twenty-five per cent of birth periods were followed by a further period in the same phase.
- Sixty-two per cent of growth periods were succeeded by further growth, 5 per cent by revival and 9 per cent by decline. Only 24 per cent moved into maturity.
- Twelve per cent of maturity phases were followed by growth and 30 per cent by revival. Only 9 per cent went into decline.
- Twenty-three per cent of revival periods were followed by maturity and 8 per cent by decline.
- Decline was continued in only 17 per cent of the succeeding periods but by revival in 42 per cent of cases and growth 7 per cent (but note that there were only 16 periods, in total, of decline).

Miller and Friesen conclude that 'aside from a tendency to remain within a given phase there is at least some tendency to follow the lifecycle' and 'while the lifecycle pattern is roughly born out, it merely represents a very rough central tendency rather than an evolutionary imperative'.

Even these rather modest statements are not provided with strong support from Drazin and Kazanjian (1990), when they apply a fairly sophisticated technique, the del procedure, to the Miller and Friesen database. Much hinges on the importance that is attached to periods in which no change occurs between phases. If such a lack of change is regarded as consistent with a lifecycle model then its predictive power would be reasonably strong. If, on the other hand, a continuation of periods within a phase is regarded as totally inconsistent, the predictive power of lifecycle models would be virtually lost and, if a compromise position is adopted, the predictive power would remain weak.

As proponents of lifecycle theories are not so foolish as to offer themselves as hostages to fortune by attaching a length of time to successive phases a long period in the same phase need not be cited as a refutation of such theories, though it might give rise to some doubts. However, when Drazin and Kazanjian (1990) state that:

It is important to note that in Miller and Friesen's data, those firms that remained in the same phase all underwent very significant organizational transitions in strategy-making, strategy, structure and environment, but still remained in the same phase of the lifecycle.

they were providing evidence, apparently unconsciously, against the validity of organizational lifecycle models because these transitions were occurring *in spite of*, not *because of* the phases experienced by the companies in the sample. Hence, factors other than growth rates would appear to be driving many important elements within the companies.

Regardless of the view that is taken of how non-movement of periods between phases, the five-phase organization cycle model would not appear to explain Miller and Friesen's data as well as three- or four-phase models, though a clear picture does not emerge of which of these offers the superior predictive ability. In the four-phase model the decline phase is omitted and, in the three-phase, the decline and revival phases.

Kazanjian (1988) produces a limited version of an organization lifecycle model when he considers whether the types of problem which a company faces are linked to its stage[4] in the cycle, drawing his sample from small and medium sized high technology companies. He finds only limited support for his model. Firms, in Stage I, 'Conception and Development', as was expected, put heavy emphasis on product and technology development and on raising capital. Those in Stage III, 'Growth', put more emphasis, than firms at other stages, on sales and marketing. The hypothesis that firms at Stage II, 'Commercialization', would 'rate problems associated with production start-up, vendor relations, facilities and field support of the product higher than will firms in other stages' was not provided with much support and only a little more than firms in Stage IV, 'Stability', being the most concerned with problems centring on 'profitability, internal controls and future sources of growth'.

As Kazanjian points out, his results provide the further insight that strategic issues, the quality of the management and non-managerial workforce, and the generation of sales are important across all stages. He also points out that his sample generally enjoyed high rates of growth (it was drawn from a list supplied by venture capitalists) so that the extent that his results can be extrapolated to less successful high technology firms, or small to medium sized enterprises (SMEs) in general, can only be resolved by further research.

The lack of any strong evidence for organization lifecycles is confirmed by Birley and Westhead (1990), who based their study on

249 small UK firms. They looked for patterns within a broad range of internal and external factors but did not find any relationship between any patterns and the size of businesses in their sample. If it is assumed that, when considered cross-sectionally, the behaviour of larger firms would be demonstrated by smaller if they catch up in size, there would not appear to be any obvious progression.

CONCLUDING REMARKS

In the strongest version of organization lifecycle models firms would inevitably pass through successive stages and there would be little scope for their management to control what was happening. This is undoubtedly to create a straw man but the emphasis of empirical research has been the existence or otherwise of patterns within firm characteristics rather than on the consequences of not conforming to those patterns. Hence, repercussions are not spelt out, for instance, from not changing the management structure as the company grows in size. The benefits to strategic planning, therefore, are limited to providing insights into the processes that the management of firms can expect to experience. These would allow the changes to be anticipated and to be managed more smoothly.

Unfortunately, the evidence is not particularly persuasive that it is possible to predict stages related to company size. Of course firms experience a host of changes in a host of respects but these need not be the result of changes in their size. This is not to say, however, that it is not helpful to management to understand the stresses that growth can bring and to consider how these might be alleviated.

11

THE RELATIVE IMPORTANCE OF INFLUENCES ON PERFORMANCE: THE CASE OF INSTRUMENTATION[1]

Earlier chapters have discussed the theory and evidence on the relationship between the performance of small firms and a whole host of factors. The list of possible influences on performance need not have ended there.[2] Indeed, given that some small firms will have been affected by such diverse factors as the Gulf war, attitude of a receptionist or the mid-life crisis of the owner, the list need never have ended. A pertinent question to both the management of small firms, and to public policy makers, is what is the relative importance of these influences? The answer would provide some indication of where attention would most fruitfully be focused.

The reasons why such an answer is not readily forthcoming from the literature is that most studies, with the notable exception of Birley and Westhead (1990), either consider only a narrow range of variables or, if they are more wide-ranging, consider each factor separately, sometimes, for instance, making a series of univariate comparisons between high and low performers, variously defined. In the latter case it may be possible to infer from levels of statistical significance where the differences between high and low performers are most marked, but this may provide little indication of which variables have the most influence on performance.[3]

Matters are not improved very much if the trawl of the literature is widened to encompass influences on the performance of new ventures.[4] These are not synonymous with small firms because they include subsidiaries of larger companies. It would be highly surprising if these were not provided with advantages over independents of the same size in terms of factors such as expertise, perceived reliability and

125

access to distribution networks, as well as the generous payback periods commonly provided by head offices to their new ventures. Hence, the influences on their performance may provide little insight into those on the performance of small independents.

If this reservation is heroically suspended studies on the factors associated with the success of new ventures suffer from the same weaknesses associated with considering variables sequentially. It is simply not possible to infer the relative importance of the various factors which would appear to be correlated with high levels of performance. Indeed, their methodology does not allow Sandberg and Hofer (1987) to conclude 'The interactive effects of industry structure, strategy and the entrepreneur had a far greater impact on new venture performance than any of these variables in isolation'.[5]

Similarly, it would not have been valid had Macmillan and Day (1987) (which they did not) drawn any conclusions from the differences in performance, as measured by market share and return on investment, between companies scoring high and low on dimensions such as relative sales promotion and relative sales force. Hobson and Morrison (1983) employ bar charts to show the relationship of various factors with market share four years after entry. It would appear that the highest shares were achieved by ventures entering markets that subsequently exhibited the most dramatic rates of growth but it would be stretching the data somewhat to conclude that this had the greatest impact on the achievement of market-share.

A further reason why univariate comparisons may not produce an accurate picture of the actual influence on performance of each variable is that this would require an absence of strong relationships between the explanatory (i.e. non-performance) variables, an issue which will be discussed more fully later. Some attempts have been made, however, to establish how performance might be affected by some such interactions. Covin and Slevin (1989), in looking at relationships between type of company, market structure and strategy concluded that in 'hostile' environments small companies that fared best had 'organic' structures. Robinson and Pearce's (1988) study of the relationship between the benefits from planning and type of strategy pursued has been reported in Chapter 7. Bradburd and Ross (1989) found some support for the conventional wisdom that the advantages from size are most likely to be eroded where markets are heterogeneous, providing opportunities for small firms to carve out appropriate niches.

This chapter is based upon an ambitious study which encompassed all of the major management disciplines, the education levels of owners and workforce and the market conditions within the segments served by the companies in its sample. The study had three objectives:

1 To consider all of the variables together, to identify which would appear to have the greatest impact on performance.
2 To establish the relative importance of the management disciplines, compared to each other and to education levels within small firms and to market conditions.
3 Within each of the sets of management, education and market condition variables to identify which would appear to be the most important in affecting performance and in what way.

METHODOLOGY

To achieve objective (1) an 'all possible subsets' regression routine was adopted in which the explanatory power[6] of, quite literally, all possible combinations of the explanatory variables was compared. Stepwise procedures, sometimes dismissed as simply 'data-mining', are regarded with far less favour in economics than in some other disciplines but the method employed in this study probably avoids their major weaknesses[7] with the exception that results may prove sample specific. To test for this, the regressions were re-run on sub-samples of observations, randomly chosen. The results were not usually significantly different from those derived from the full sample and certainly the thrust of the conclusions remained unaltered.

In order to achieve objectives (2) and (3) separate regressions were run on the sets of variables relating to each of the management disciplines, to education levels and to market conditions. The relative importance of each set in influencing performance was established through comparison of R^2 and of the variables within each set conventionally from the size of coefficients and 't' statistics.

Running separate regressions in this way is highly unusual. It would only be valid if the variables included in one set were not related in some way to variables in another, otherwise the results would be rendered unreliable by 'omitted variable' bias. The most straightforward of such types of relationship, where two explanatory variables demonstrate a high degree of correlation, was largely absent from the data set. The correlation matrix showed only twenty-six simple correlations of 0.4 or above out of a total possible of approximately 1,600. In all cases if a variable was replaced with one with which it was correlated, the replacement variable had an insignificant 't' value in any regression.

Unfortunately, for regression analysis in general, as well as for this study in particular, multicollinearity (i.e. relationships between explanatory variables) can take far more subtle forms than would be suggested by a simple correlation matrix. For instance, suppose a variable is not related directly to either of two other variables, taken separately, but to combinations of those variables. This would not be reflected by a correlation matrix. Similarly, neither would a situation where a dependent variable were not affected by a particular variable on its own but only when a third were present, the role of which might be purely catalytic, with the latter value having no direct influence itself on the dependent variable.

Examples of such subtlety are not hard to find outside the pages of econometrics textbooks. It might well have been the influences of the factors incorporated in this study were contingent on the values of some of the other factors or on how these were combined.

To test fully whether this was the case would have required each explanatory variable to have been regressed against all other possible combinations of the other explanatory variables, a lifetime's endeavour. It was done, however, with respect to the variables generated to achieve objective (1), i.e. the most important influences on performance. They would not appear to be related to each other. Nor would variables employed in *ad hoc* regressions where a relationship between them would not have been surprising. Hence, whilst by no means ruling out the possibility that variables in one regression were related to those in another, there is no obvious evidence of this, nor would its danger appear any greater than would confront any study, and not just if it were employing statistical techniques, which attempted to establish the strength of a fresh set of variables on a factor on which previous studies had discovered other influences.

CHOICE OF VARIABLES

Personal

As intimated in Chapter 6, attempting to assess the relationship between the personality, values, beliefs and objectives of principal decision-makers and the performance of their firms is fraught with difficulties which may be regarded, indeed, as unsurmountable. The broad problems are two-fold. Personality and value systems are concepts which are neither simple nor straightforward. People may demonstrate different types of behaviour and possess apparently inconsistent sets of attitudes depending upon the situation. Serial killers may be pacifists in wartime, which may be simply a reversal of the conventional wisdom that it is wrong to kill someone one knows but quite right, on the orders of one's government, to kill complete strangers. Rather more mundane examples of multifacedness are so common that one is spoilt for choice. The tyrant with fellow directors may be indulgent with junior staff or friends and family. In that case describing his personality is clearly problematic. Similarly, what conclusions should be drawn about the attention to detail displayed by the meticulous planner at work who is hopeless at managing her own finances, the commonly observed 'cobbler with holes in her shoes' phenomenon?

The sides of their personality that people display will also depend upon personal chemistry. It would be totally trivial, if it were not apparently ignored by many researchers on personality–performance relationships, that the image projected is not independent of the interaction with the person receiving it. Again the question arises of what actually constitutes personality.

Even in the absence of such ambiguity or multifacedness research in the area of personality and value systems may not prove very reliable. Whatever method is adopted to establish what people think – asking them questions, inviting them to respond to value statements, to give their opinion on hypothetical situations, and so on – runs the strong risk that responses may reflect what respondents would like the researcher to believe about them, or what they would like to believe about themselves or what they genuinely believe about themselves, but may serve as no guide to actual behaviour. Otherwise the religious would be expected to be kinder and more moral than the atheistic, which experience would not suggest to be true.

In the light of these difficulties it was decided to focus on the education levels of chief executives and their employees which, at least, can be established fairly unambiguously. Specifically:

1	Whether the founder, owner or chief executive had ever attended a short management course.
2,3 and 4	Whether the chief executive had a PhD, BSc or Higher National Diploma (HND).
5 and 6	The proportion of employees with any level of higher education or with an HND.

Strategy

The variables chosen represent a mix between those that might generally be expected to be important to the performance of a small firm and those that might be influential on the performance of small firms specifically operating in the instrumentation sector:

7   The percentage of sales from the most important product.

      This was designed to indicate the breadth of product portfolio. For a small firm, with its limited marketing capabilities, the trade-off is between concentrating its efforts on a few key products, with the inherent risk that demand will not prove sustainable, and maintaining a more balanced portfolio, that might imply spreading marketing effort too thinly. There may also be a trade-off between the benefits from economies of scale of a limited portfolio and economies of scope from breadth of product-range.

8, 9,   Whether the marketing strategy was targeted by: the end-
10,11,   user sector in which the principal product would be
and 12   employed (e.g. chemicals); the joint product to which the instrument would be attached (e.g. a mass-spectrometer); the application of the instrument (e.g. temperature control); the features of the instrument, irrespective of the above (e.g. user-friendliness); geographical region.

Small firms are usually advised to pursue a niche strategy but this is not only fairly self-evident but, in practice, it is difficult for a small firm not to find itself specializing in a particular segment of a market, if not a niche within that segment. What is not self-evident is the segment, even less the niche, that it would be most sensible for a small firm to attempt to occupy. The above represent some of the more important ways in which instrumentation might be segmented. Disaggregation to the level of niches, for instance particular types of joint products or applications, was not feasible with the size of the sample in the study.

13   Whether the underlying strategy was of low cost or high
and 14   quality.

Regardless of choice of segment, firms must aim for a place on the price–quality spectrum, on the assumption that it will rarely prove possible to achieve the best of both worlds, i.e. low price and high quality.

Financial control

15   The percentage shortfall on the intended volume of borrowing over the last five years.

If they are to avoid complete reliance on their own resources or on capital provided by friends and relatives, owners must possess at least some ability to negotiate with the capital market, specifically banks (none of our sample had had recourse to venture capitalists). Failure to raise any money at its inception could mean that the company never leaves the 'bright idea' stage. The expectation at the start of the study was that the most successful firms would have had the smallest shortfall from their intended size of loan.

16   Whether cashflows were forecast: yearly; quarterly.
and 17
18   Whether records of cashflow were updated monthly or
and 19   quarterly.

The management of cashflow is normally regarded as important to a small firm. It is perfectly possible for a profitable firm to fail because its management was taken by surprise by its levels of inflows and outflows, though this danger would be far less severe if banks were perfectly efficient, as unexpected deficits would readily be covered on the strength of future receipts. The variables employed in this study were intended to reflect the foresight displayed in the planning of cashflow and the accuracy of cashflow data available to management.

20   The number of days before a bill was typically paid.
21   The number of days before an invoice was typically dispatched.

Other things being equal it is better to pay bills as late as possible, and receive payment as early, but this ignores the ill-will that such a hard-nosed policy can generate.

It may also make the planning of cashflow more difficult. Either factor could have been the cause of the strong positive relationship, recorded in Chapter 5, between the probability of failure among small firms in construction, and the length of time they took to pay their bills. It would not be surprising if some similar relationship existed with other measures of performance.

22   Whether procedures were typically formalized in writing.

Surprisingly, given the thrust of previous work reported in Chapter 7 almost a half of interviewees claimed to some degree of formalization in their planning. Chapter 7 also reported the quite sharp division of opinion as to whether such formalization would be likely to make very much difference to the performance of a small firm.

Marketing

23   Whether the company carried out surveys among: cus-
and 24   tomers; distributors.

The conventional wisdom is fairly unambiguous that some sort of market research is likely to be superior to intuition as a source of information.

25, 26   Whether the interviewee believed his products were pur-
and 27   chased because of the quality of: the product; the service; the delivery times.

This question was introduced to establish which aspect of instruments provides the highest return to an investment in quality. Given the self-delusion which managers normally display towards the quality of their products this must be regarded as a very rough and ready measure of actual sources of quality.

28   The number employed in the marketing function.

This was intended as an indication of the company's commitment to marketing.

29   The advertising to sales ratio.
30   The proportion of sales in 1989 to current customers.

The latter was intended to establish the importance to the company of repeat purchasing. A heavy reliance may indicate that the company has a sufficiently sound product that it does not need to market proactively or, conversely, a conservative reluctance to securing new customers. Similarly, heavy advertising may reflect dynamism or an absence of customer loyalty.

Management of innovation

It would be expected a priori that the management of the innovation process would be important for success in the instrumentation sector. This would be confirmed by previous studies (Rothwell *et al.* 1974, Von Hippel, 1976; 1977, and Madique and Zirger, 1985) which have also provided some pointers to the appropriate specification of the variables:

31   Whether products were typically launched from a programme for research and development (R&D) carried out without regard to signals from the market as to what the outcome should be.

32   Whether the design of products was typically specified by customers.

33   Whether they would typically work closely with customers in the development of their products.

The expectation was that firms that were responsive to signals from the market in the research and development of new products would be more successful than those who either relied on their intuition as to what was likely to prove popular, or than those that carried out research without close regard to commercial considerations.

34   Whether they would regard themselves as essentially subcontractors.

The assumption behind this question was that acting as a subcontractor reduced the need to carry out R&D but significantly reduced the company's scope for charging premium prices.

35   The percentage of sales from products launched since 1983.

This was introduced as a measure of the extent that the company had introduced changes into its product line. The expectation was that it was desirable that it should have done so though, with the recognition, that such changes might be unnecessary for companies with a demonstrably winning product.

36   Percentage of sales spent on R&D.

37   Number employed in R&D.

38   Number of patents taken since 1983.

These were intended to indicate the strength of commitment of companies to R&D.

Operations management

39   Average throughput time of the major product.

40   Average stock turn (i.e. the ratio of stock to sales).

These were introduced as measures, albeit rather crude, of operational efficiency.

41   Whether using computer aided design.

42   Whether using materials requirement planning.

43   Whether using Just in Time.

At the time of the study these were regarded as fairly state of the art operations management techniques.

44   Number of customers in total.

In industrial markets the number of customers need not serve as any indication of volume of demand but a highly concentrated customer base does render a company vulnerable to buyer power. On the other hand, a limited portfolio of companies is easier to manage, especially where companies work closely with their customers.

45   Percentage of sales from servicing.

To the extent that customers will usually ask the original supplier of a product to carry out its servicing this activity might be described as fairly captive. Servicing is not normally associated, however, with high mark-ups.

46   Whether competitors in the segment served by the major product were typically bigger.

Marked differences in the size of companies serving the same markets can normally only arise in the absence of economies of scale or, in the presence of economies if the benefits from size have not yet been realized or if small firms have recognized the disadvantages they face, but consider either that the rewards justified facing the disadvantages or that they had no alternative to confronting them.

THE SAMPLE

The sample of small firms was drawn from the population of firms that:

- In 1983, were independent, operated solely in instrumentation and had a labour force of 200 or less.
- In 1988, had remained independent and in instrumentation. No constraints were imposed on their size in the later period.

In fact the average age within the sample was twenty-three years in 1988 (minimum six, maximum seventy-five), and the average number of employees forty-nine, (minimum four, maximum 143).

The sample was drawn from the FAME database from which the data on performance were drawn.

RESULTS

Table 11.1 Influences on return on sales

	Coefficient	Standardized Coefficient
Market targeted by end-user	25.56	0.73
	(6.5)	
Underlying strategy of quality	15.83	0.54
	(5.1)	
Chief Executive had an HND	10.15	0.43
	(4.4)	
Time taken to pay bills	−0.19	−0.35
	(−3.6)	
Shortfall in amount borrowed	0.34	0.34
	(3.6)	
If competition in the segment served by its major product were typically bigger	−5.79	−0.25
	(−2.5)	
Carried out customer surveys	5.36	0.20
	(2.0)	
Percentage of sales spent on advertising	−0.86	−0.14
	(−1.5)	

*Numbers in brackets are 't' statistics $\overline{R}^2 = 0.71$ F = 13.8

Most important influences on profitability

Focus by end user

Firms adopting a strategy of focusing on particular end-user markets enjoyed the highest returns on sales and this would appear to have had a greater impact on profitability than any of the other variables in the study. It would seem that the route for success for a small firm in instrumentation is a to have a clear view as to the markets in which its products will be employed.

High quality

The second most important influence on profitability would appear to be the position on which the firms were located on the price–cost spectrum. Irrespective of the direction of the focus of their strategies, or conceivably of whether there was any such focus, the highest returns were earned by firms located at the high quality end of the spectrum. Given the scope for benefiting from research and development which is offered by this sector, and the inability of small firms to exploit economies of scale, this should not come as a complete surprise.

Taking both aspects of strategy together would suggest, albeit rather weakly, that the successful firms would have been located in Robinson and Pearce's (1988) cluster 4 in that they would appear to have aimed for 'extensive customer service/building industry reputation/high priced market segments/avoid price competition/avoid low-priced market segments'.

The thrust of the results did not suggest that the most successful firms attached quite the importance identified by Robinson and Pearce (*op. cit.*) to product innovation and development, except in so far as targeting specific types of end-users, and pursuing a policy of high quality, implies a commitment to these factors.

Education

The interviewees were exceptionally well educated for the chief executives of small firms. One had a PhD, twenty-eight had degrees and the remaining ten, HNDs or equivalent. It was the last group that saw their companies earning the highest returns. This would not be consistent with Jovanovich's (1982) model of small-firm failure, which would imply that the performance of such firms would be significantly improved with increases in the volume of their human capital, which the possession of degrees by their senior management would presumably help them to achieve, or with the results of Bates' (1990) empirical testing of this model. It would, however, be quite consistent with conclusions from Chapter 5 as to the factors associated with failure within the construction sector. The few owners with degrees all experienced failure, whereas those with ordinary level GCE or equivalent had a higher probability of survival than those without any formal qualifications. Although the results of two studies, one on failure, the other on profitability, hardly constitute comprehensive, even less, conclusive evidence there is clearly a suggestion that the possession of a degree does not put its recipient in a better position either to ensure his company's survival or a higher level of profitability.

Cashflow management

The time taken to pay bills was strongly and negatively correlated with profitability. Though late payment of bills would provide the obvious opportunity to earn interest, the advantage from this would appear to be outweighed by less obvious disadvantages, for instance the ill-will that might be generated with suppliers, which might bear sour fruit if supplies needed to be rationed, or the difficulty of planning expenditure that might accompany constant delays, particularly if these are of haphazard lengths. It may well be that efficient managers do everything promptly, including paying their bills, or that those in less profitable companies perceive little alternative to putting off payment to the last minute (though that does not mean that it would nevertheless, not be in the interests of the more profitable to delay payment). Whatever the explanation it is surely not without significance that the results of the study on failure among small firms in construction found late payment of bills to be highly correlated with the probability of failure. It should, moreover, be emphasized that the studies of the two sectors were carried out quite independently, differing in the identity of their fieldworkers, the period during which they carried out their interviews and in the contents of the questionnaires.

Relations with bank

There was a positive relationship between profitability and the difference between the amount requested and amount received from banks during the previous five years. This is certainly surprising. The measure was intended to indicate the chief executive's capability at negotiating with the capital market, with the sign, therefore, expected to be negative. The reverse would suggest that it has been the most profitable firms that have experienced most difficulty in raising what their management believed to be the most appropriate amount of money, which might be regarded as some reflection on the efficiency of the capital market.

Market conditions

Firms typically facing larger competitors achieved lower returns than those whose competitors were the same size or smaller. This may, of course, simply be the result of economies of scale but such a conclusion provides no insights into whether these came as a surprise to the owners of small firms, implying an ignorance about an important dimension of market structure – for a small firm, perhaps the most important dimension – or, if the disadvantages they would face, were known in advance, why the decision was nevertheless made to face them.

Market research

It would appear advisable to carry out market research among potential and current customers. Firms doing so enjoyed higher returns. This is exactly as might be expected.

Advertising

Profitability was negatively related to the advertising to sales ratio. This was not expected but, nevertheless, certainly should not be construed as counter-intuitive. The most profitable firms in our sample apparently relied on other means than advertising to promote the sales of their products, perhaps reputation or customer loyalty, but its form must remain a matter of conjecture.

It should be noted that its low 't' value might have led to the omission of this variable but the selection procedure employed was specifically not based on levels of 't' statistics.

This study has attempted to identify the factors which have had the greatest influence on the profitability of small firms operating in the instrumentation sector. The only similar study, would appear to be that by Birley and Westhead (1990). Their sample of small businesses was much larger and more broadly based than that employed in this study, though their stepwise procedure did not generate a set of variables which explained more than 14 per cent of the variation between businesses in perceived relative profitability. Their final model would suggest that the most important associations were positively with the company's age and negatively with whether they had 'received finance from a large number of sources (not including overdraft facilities from banks)'. It is not clear what inference should be drawn from the latter relationship.

An earlier stage in the stepwise process suggested management training and holding 'regular and frequent meetings with their customers and suppliers' had also benefited the profitability of the companies in their study. The first result would be consistent with the Jovanovich (*op. cit.*) model of small firm survival, the latter with that of Dollinger (1984) of the importance to the performance of small firms of the 'boundary spanning' activities of the chief executives.

Most important influences on growth

This section is based on the premise that the growth rates displayed

Table 11.2 Influences on proportionate growth

	Coefficient	Standardized Coefficient
Proportion of employees with higher education	2.03 (2.3)*	0.55
Market targeted by end-user	62.60 (2.39)	0.36
Underlying strategy of quality	62.11 (1.75)	0.32
If competitors in the segment served by the major product were typically bigger	–28.55 (–1.3)	–0.19
Constant	–29.66 (–1.03)	0

by the firms in the sample were influenced by the various factors encompassed by the study and not vice versa. This would be false if the process of changing turnover led to changes in any of these factors; in other words if growth was a cause not a result of the variables included in the regression. With the exception of the first of the variables discussed below it would be stretching the imagination to envisage how the direction of causation could be anything but as assumed.

What is quite striking is how the influences on growth would appear to have been very similar to those on profitability though their combined explanatory power, as reflected in the $\overline{R}^2$, was much lower. Market research does not, however, appear to have been one of the most important influences on growth. Indeed, as will be discussed later, it does not appear to have had any relationship with growth. This is certainly surprising and would not be consistent with results of the attempt by Storey, Watson and Wynarczyk (1989) to identify the factors distinguishing a sample of twenty high growth small firms from a sample of firms of the same number displaying only average growth. A greater emphasis on market intelligence would appear to have been one such factor.

Education of the workforce

The variable with the strongest relationship with growth was the proportion of the workforce with HNDs or certificates or with degrees. It is perfectly plausible that the increase in volume of their human capital represented by the education levels of their workforce enabled the firms to achieve the higher levels of growth. Alternatively, as firms grew they recruited a greater proportion of highly educated staff, facilitating but not causing the expansion.

Focus and quality

It would appear that adopting a strategy of focusing on a particular end-user market and of producing high quality, rather than low cost, products was associated with higher rates of growth as well as with higher profits. The message would seem clear, whatever measure of performance is adopted.

Market conditions

Facing a bigger competitor in the segment served by the major product would appear not only to affect profitability detrimentally but growth, though with the caveat that the 't' statistic on this variable is low. This conclusion would not be consistent with what appears to be the thrust of the results from studies of factors associated with new venture performance based on the PIMS[8] database. Hofer and Sandberg (1987), in their review of such studies, state the PIMS data:

> Clearly showed that new venture entry was more successful when the entries that were entered had a dominant competitor (i.e. one competitor with >49 per cent share) than when the largest existing competitor had less than 25 per cent share

but did not cite any specific references to support this assertion.[9] They may have been thinking of Hobson and Morrison's (1983) study of influences on market-share four years post entry, though their results were not presented in a way that enabled such precise conclusions to be drawn about the nature of the relationship. In trying to explain what might prima facie is a rather counter-intuitive conclusion, Hofer and Sandberg (op. cit.) agree with Hobson and Morrison (op. cit.) that it may belie the increased competition that may accompany an equal distribution of market-shares, but consider more likely that a dominant producer implies a greater weakness among the remaining firms.

It is clearly important to know whether the relative size of incumbents in a segment has any impact on the likelihood of success of small firms entering this segment. It would certainly appear that bigger firms will usually have a negative affect on profitability but there is less certainty about the effect on growth. The results of this study are consistent with those reported in Chapter 12 from the STRATOS study but not those of the PIMS data. The reason may simply be that the latter refer to different variables: their samples are drawn from the subsidiaries of larger companies and market-share is not synonymous with company size.

Comparing the importance of sets of variables

Profitability

Adopting the criteria that a set of variables should be regarded as having some influence collectively on return on sales if its $\overline{R}^2$ in a separate regression were 0.1 or above, leads to the conclusion that this measure of performance was affected about equally by marketing and financial variables (R^2 of 0.24 and 0.21, respectively) followed in importance by strategic variables (0.14). The education level, innovation, operations management and market conditions variables apparently had no impact collectively on profitability.

Growth

Change in sales was most strongly associated with financial variables (R^2 = 0.39), strategic (0.28) and education levels (0.19). As many factors can be affected by a firm's change in size, direction of causation is less straightforward to establish than in the regressions on profitability. It would seem more likely that efficiency in the financial management of a firm facilitated growth rather than caused it and the same conclusion can probably be reached regarding the volume of human capital embodied in a firm as implied by the education level variables. In other words, firms may not have grown if they had not exhibited efficient financial management or if they had not increased their volume of human capital but doing so perhaps approached a necessary rather than sufficient condition for growth.

The adoption of appropriate strategies, on the other hand, can realistically be expected to directly affect a firm's volume of sales or the price at which it is sold. Collectively the marketing, innovation, operations management and market conditions variables would not appear to have been associated with the growth of the companies.

It should be emphasized that these results do not contradict the results of the attempt to identify the most important influences on performance. The possession of HNDs by owners, and carrying out market research, continued to have a positive effect on profitability, and competing against a bigger company and relying on advertising to generate sales, a negative. Similarly, lower growth was also achieved by companies facing a bigger competitor.

However, the overall explanatory power of the pertinent regressions was low, reflecting the reduction in the value of the $\bar{R}^2$ with the addition of each variable that is non-statistically significant.

What is certainly surprising are the sets of variables that would not appear to have been associated, to any great extent, with profitability or growth. The most notable of these would be market conditions. It would seem intuitively obvious, as well as consistent with economic theory, that the immediate environment in which a firm operates will have an impact on its performance but this is not confirmed by the results of this study. It may be that interviewees had inaccurate perceptions of the market conditions they faced, with the bias unrelated to how well their companies performed, which would account for the lack of any apparent relationships. However, the change in total sales within the segment served by the firm's major product was derived from published statistics; no subjectivity was involved.

The conclusion that the performance of the firms in this study did not mirror the growth within their principal served market would not be inconsistent with the statistic provided by Leigh *et al.* (1991) that only 50 per cent of high growth firms in their study described their markets as 'strong or growing', though using the same database Smallbone *et al.* (1993) did suggest that rapid growth combined with consistent profitability was a little more likely to be achieved in 'benign' rather than 'hostile' markets.

The evidence on the factors associated with the success of new ventures, including subsidiaries of big companies, is not overwhelming on the importance of growth in sales within the total market. It does not emerge as crucial from Hofer and Sandberg's (1987) survey of the literature. Hobson and Morrison (1983) did conclude that market share four years post-entry was related to change in total market sales post-entry, but not pre-entry. Stuart and Abbetti (1987), on the other hand, found success more likely in stable than growing markets, whereas Biggadike (1979) found the highest returns (actually smallest losses) came from serving markets with moderate growth, though the next best was from high growth.

The thrust of the results from this and other studies would seem to be that the success of a small firm will depend far more upon the policies it adopts than the buoyancy of the markets in which it operates. Internal efficiency would appear more important than the general state of its environment, though small firms should, nevertheless, avoid competition with companies that are bigger.

The absence should not go unremarked of any relationship of either measure of performance with the sets of variables designed to reflect approaches to the management of operations and of innovation. The questions asked as regards the adoption of what were regarded at the outset of the project as best practices in operations management, were straightforward and unambiguous, with definitions provided, where appropriate, by the interviewer. Assuming, therefore, that the questions have been answered reasonably accurately, efficiency in operations management would not appear to make any difference to success. The issues addressed on the management of the innovation process were somewhat more vague but, given the conventional wisdom that this aspect of management is important to success in instrumentation, some relationships might nevertheless have been expected to be discernible.

The apparent importance of the set of marketing variables in influencing profitability is not surprising but lack of association with growth was rather counter-intuitive though the testimony from previous studies to the importance of marketing in achieving high growth rates is not overwhelming. Storey, Watson and Wynarczyk (1989) found the chief executives of their fastest growing firms were more likely than those of companies with average rates of growth to have had a background in marketing and to carry out market and competitor intelligence. Brooksbank *et al.* (1992) found evidence for the importance of marketing from in-depth interviews and from their postal survey. Hobson and Morrison (1983), in considering factors associated with market-share four years post-entry, did not reach any strong conclusions regarding the role of marketing but Macmillan and Day (1987) were more positive about the association of the market-shares of new ventures and various marketing variables such as relative advertising and salesforce expenditure.

Relative importance of variables

From their 't' statistics it is possible to identify which variables have had any influence on performance and, from the values of their standardized coefficients, their relative importance. This will only be accurate in the absence of multicollinearity with other variables within the same regression model and with variables within other sets of variables. As stated earlier no such multicollinearity is obvious but its presence would need to be quite acute before the thrust of the following results was invalidated. Not surprisingly, in models with low overall explanatory power, only the variables identified in the stepwise procedure as having the strongest influences on performance were statistically significant.

Profitability

Marketing The importance of market research was reinforced. Firms carrying out market research with either customers or distributors enjoyed far higher levels of return on sales than those not carrying out market research. The more profitable firms were less likely to rely on repeat purchases and advertising to secure their sales and to regard speed of delivery as their selling point. The number employed in marketing did not appear to make any difference, either way, to profitability nor did making a particular virtue of after-sales service.

Financial management

The most profitable firms, as suggested earlier, suffered the biggest shortfalls in their intended borrowing and paid their bills most promptly. It would seem to make most difference to profitability to forecast, and to update, the cashflow position on a quarterly basis. Updating such information on a monthly basis or forecasting yearly did not appear to have any effect on profitability, nor did dispatching invoices promptly or formalizing information systems.

Strategic management

The model was strongly driven by adopting strategies of focusing on a particular end-user and of selling high quality products. There was some suggestion that higher performance was achieved by concentrating on a narrow range of products. Limiting the regression to these three variables alone dramatically raised the R^2. All other variables would appear to have been unrelated to profitability.

Growth

Financial management

There was a strong relationship between growth and updating information quarterly on cashflow. Companies updating such information on a monthly basis also enjoyed higher rates of growth than those firms that, by implication, were only aware of their cashflow position longer than three months earlier. It would seem that fast growing companies must be fully on top of their cashflow position. The fast growing firms also dispatched their invoices earliest but the high negative correlation with the time taken to pay bills was not repeated, nor with the percentage shortfall on borrowing. However, as with profitability the optimal period over which to make forecasts of cashflow would appear to be quarterly and formalization of procedures would appear to be irrelevant.

Strategic management

The importance of targeting by end-user market was reinforced. Focusing by application had a positive, and statistically significant (at 10 per cent), relationship with growth, whereas targeting by joint product or product attributes had a negative impact and targeting by geographical region, no impact. The adoption of low cost strategies was associated with the lowest rates of growth.

Education levels

Firms employing a high proportion of staff with higher education levels experienced the highest rates of growth as did these whose chief executive had a degree. The possession of PhD, HND or management course experience would not appear to have made any difference to growth.

CONCLUDING REMARKS

Only further research will reveal if the conclusions from this study would be valid for sectors other than instrumentation. It would clearly be of great significance if the highest levels of performance, in terms of growth and profitability, were generally achieved by small firms with a focus on a specific end-user market, producing at the high quality end of the price–quality spectrum and avoiding competition with bigger companies and if the relative importance of categories of variables (indeed absence of importance in some notable cases) were maintained across sectors. The extent that this is confirmed by the results of the more extensive STRATOS study will be discussed in the next chapter.

Interestingly, the apparent lack of a simple relationship of profitability with level of owner-education, the inverse relationship with time taken to pay bills, and positive relationship between growth and skill levels within the workforce, are all consistent with the relationships between these variables and probability of failure within construction, reported in Chapter 5. Some of the factors that assist in achieving survival may also benefit subsequent success.

12

INFLUENCES ON GROWTH: AN INTERNATIONAL COMPARISON[1]

One of the most exciting, certainly comprehensive studies, of the small- and medium-sized firm sector has been carried out by the STRATOS (an approximate acronym for 'strategic orientation of small and medium sized enterprises') project team, headed by Ingolf Bamberger (The Stratos Group, 1990).[2] It consisted of carrying out personal interviews with 1,132 managers, by implication usually owners, of small- and medium-sized enterprises (SMEs) in Austria, Belgium, Finland, France, West Germany, Switzerland, The Netherlands and the United Kingdom, operating in food, clothing/footwear and electronics. Eighty-six per cent of firms had workforces of less than 100, and none more than 500.

Much of the study is concerned with the values and objectives of interviewees. The former were inferred from the relative importance attached to various statements, for instance 'business before family', 'who carries out decisions should share in making them' and 'professional bodies should only provide assistance'. Patterns within these responses were then interpreted as reflecting whether interviewees were 'all-rounders', 'pioneers', 'organizers' and 'routineers'. Such a methodology has a respectable pedigree in psychology, though comments made in Chapters 6 and 11 of this book reflect a scepticism about its validity. It clearly rests on the assumption that beliefs can be inferred from responses to statements and that the relationships between beliefs and responses, and between beliefs and behaviour, can be assumed in advance. If responses to statements are not just a matter of chance or of whim on the part of interviewees, and if correlations between responses would remain robust between different samples of interviewees drawn from the sample of country-sector populations, it does not necessarily follow that beliefs reflect responses or that beliefs determine behaviour in a straightforward manner. To reiterate and, no doubt, unduly labour the points made earlier, it is by no means obvious that the responses of psychotics would necessarily imply a greater willingness to commit violence than might be found within, say, a convent, nor that mafia bosses, who allegedly perceive themselves as patriotic and, respectable members of the property owning classes, would necessarily provide responses suggesting a stronger tolerance of crime than might be the case with professors of criminology.

Luckily, for the purposes of this book, within the thirty pages of the questionnaire there were many questions, the answers to which offered far less scope for uncertainty as to interpretation. Some of these related to factors, internal or external to the firm, discussed in earlier chapters as possible influences on performance.

Proportionate growth, 1980–83, has been chosen as the most reliable measure of performance. Profitability would have been a suitable additional measure but differences in accounting conventions between countries render it unreliable in international studies.

The remainder of this chapter will discuss methodology, choice of variables and results.

METHODOLOGY

Initially an attempt was made to identify the most important influences on performance by regressing the proportionate growth of each company on the levels of the factors that were quantitative (e.g. the market share held by the three largest firms in the market) and on the qualitative variables indicating to whichever of possible alternatives an affirmative response had been provided (e.g. 'Would you describe (your market) as very large/large/medium/small?').

The attempt to find a relationship on such a company by company basis proved unsuccessful. So many factors can affect the growth of an SME that it was not possible to measure the separate impact of each one.

As a second line of attack, the data were grouped into ninety-six cells (eight countries x three sectors x four size bands) and the average proportionate growth displayed in each was regressed on the average levels of each of the quantitative variables and proportion of companies in each cell providing a positive response to each of the yes/no questions. Because of the large number of variables involved a stepwise procedure, all possible subsets regression, was adopted, which identified the variables which collectively had the greatest influence on proportionate growth. The end result was a model explaining about three-quarters of the variation in growth, though only after deletion of two of the cells, both of which referred to French data. Having done this, the results proved robust when the model was re-tested on various sub-samples of cells, chosen randomly.

The improvement in explanatory power after aggregation into cells is not particularly surprising. Generally speaking, aggregation enables the influence of one factor on average on another to be identified even when that influence is slight with respect to individual cases. Attempting to predict the lifespan of an individual, for instance, on the basis of how much he smoked, his eating habits and exercise regimes would almost certainly prove less successful than if data on individuals were pooled and an attempt made to estimate effects on average lifespans of heavy smoking, high cholesterol diets and sedentary lifestyles.

CHOICE OF VARIABLES

Most of the variables extracted from the STRATOS database would be implied by the discussion of influences on performance presented in Chapters 7–10. It should be remembered, however, that it was never the intention of STRATOS to carry out this kind of exercise – indeed this is very much a bonus from the original study – so that, not surprisingly, the variables have not always been specified (i.e. the questions that were included in the survey) in a form that necessarily would be considered ideal in order to establish the reasons for different rates of growth between firms.

So little empirical work has been carried out on the influences on small firm performance, however, and the STRATOS project generated such a rich vein of information that, whatever its shortcomings, it represents an unequalled opportunity to study these influences across Europe.

Personal

Earlier chapters have discussed the importance of human capital for the survival and success of small firms. Variables were therefore selected from the STRATOS database which might be related to the volume of such capital. Age was one obvious choice, on the grounds that people gain from experience, though with the caveats that there may be an optimum age at which to run a company, as suggested by Bates (1990), or that the advantages from youth might outweigh those of age, as apparently is the case in construction. Of course, both Bates and the results discussed in Chapter 5, refer to the relationship of age to survival. It may be the case that, once a survival threshold has been jumped, the relationship may be quite different between growth and age.

Other variables which may rather obviously be related to the volume of human capital embodied in an owner would be the age at which she left full-time education, and whether she had attended any sort of management course. A less obvious choice was the occupation of the owner's father. It is well known that class is related to academic levels of achievement until, at least, the higher education stage has been reached. It is possible, because of differences in inculcated value systems, that owners from middle-class backgrounds will prove more successful in terms of the growth of their companies than those from working-class backgrounds. A contra-hypothesis would be that owners with more humble beginnings, having jumped the class barrier to start their own company, would display a greater will to succeed.

The motivation of owners represents a further personal characteristic which may influence their effectiveness at running their companies. In order to establish motivation, albeit suspending the scepticism expressed in earlier chapters about the validity of using responses to questions to provide insights into such areas, interviewees were asked to demonstrate the importance they attached (on a scale of 1–5) to financial considerations, specifically 'financial independence', 'doing better than other businessmen' and 'high levels of income'. Responses indicating a very low priority to any of these were aggregated. The regression would indicate whether such financial ambition serves as a more powerful motivator than alternatives such as power, security, establishment of a family business to be bequeathed to future generations, independence or self-fulfilment.

MARKET CHARACTERISTICS

Size of markets

Other things being equal, one would expect companies whose owners described their markets as 'large' or 'very large' to experience highest rates of growth.

Stage in 'lifecycle'

Similarly, though the results reported in the last chapter provide grounds for caution, expanding markets are likely to offer more scope for growth than static. Interviewees were asked to categorize their served markets as in an 'introduction', 'growth', 'transition from growth to maturity' or 'maturity' phase.

Seasonality

Where demand was described as 'fairly regular' it was included as a variable. Alternatives, not included in the analysis were 'seasonal' or 'irregular'. The albeit rather weak null hypothesis, was that growth would be more likely in more stable conditions.

Price elasticity

This was indicated by three variables: whether demand was perceived as 'rather sensitive to price changes', and separately, questions were put regarding the importance to competition of prices and quality, respectively. Products in markets driven by price competition are likely to be close substitutes, offering fewer options for winning market share.

Competition on quality at least offers the opportunity to small firms to make improvements that lead to growth in sales.

Concentration of buyers

This was measured in several ways: whether the company relied on 1–10 'key' customers, the number of its customers and the proportion of its sales taken by its three largest customers. Relying on a few customers for, by implication, repeat business reduces the need for marketing but increases both the risk of unexpectedly losing a significant proportion of sales and of suffering the squeezed profit margins from buyer power. The effect on growth is, however, indeterminate. If a small firm does not carry out any marketing direct to the final customer but sells to a retailer its growth will be dependent on the latter's merchandising skills. If its customer is another company, the level of sales of its products will reflect those of its customer. Whether therefore, on average, reliance on a few customers ultimately leads to a higher rate of growth than attempting to increase sales by increasing the customer base, can only be resolved empirically.

Size of main competitors

One would not expect firms of significantly different sizes to compete head-on in established markets in which size provides an advantage, either in relation to scale of output or to scope, the range of activities undertaken. Competition would be avoided by small firms occupying niches either in which size provides no advantage or which have been ignored by large firms. Competition would be most likely in markets characterized by an absence of economies of scale or of scope, or in which the potential benefits have yet to be realized or had been underestimated by small firms when making the decision to enter them. Except in the last case, whether small firms find they can grow more rapidly at the expense of large than of small will depend upon the extent of diseconomies of scale, perhaps a slowness to respond to changing condition, lack of customer care, etc.

Market share

The statistical correlation between market share and profitability is well established, at least for large firms but there is less reason for supposing a relationship between market share and growth in sales, except in so far as in a static market change in market share must, by definition, be the same as change in sales.

Exports

Whether the main product group generates most of its sales locally/regionally, nationally or throughout the world, and proportion of sales from exports, treated as four separate variables. It is not uncommon in business to argue for the desirability of expanding from local markets to national, and from national to international but there is precious little theory to underpin this. Obviously the potential for increasing sales will increase with the size of the perceived served market – the world is bigger than Manchester – but so might the level of competition that will be met, and, almost certainly, the problems that will arise from attempting to do business at a distance.

Market differentiation

Whether the needs of customers were considered as 'very differentiated' and the number of different customer groups within their served markets, were treated as two variables. Other things being equal, both would offer the greater scope for strategic marketing and hence for growth. On the other hand, if the number of customer groups is large, with the size of each numerically small, the scope for expansion by concentrating on a particular group may be more limited.

State of technology

Whether the served market involved 'very complex technology'. Although it is possible for sophisticated technology to be introduced into static or declining markets it is most likely to be associated with the exploitation of new opportunities with the expectation that firms that exploit these opportunities will enjoy the results in higher levels of growth.

Competitor behaviour

Whether there had been a 'critical change' in competitor behaviour over the previous three years. Except where this challenge had been entirely neutralized one would expect it to result in a lower level of performance.

All of the above may be described as factors external to the firm, though to varying degrees. A heavy export orientation, for instance, may have been forced by the nature of the market or may have been chosen in preference to other strategic options. Similarly, the following may be described as internal factors but with the caveat that circumstances may serve as a powerful constraint on the policies that can be adopted. Ideally, a study distinguishing between external and internal influences on performance would hold constant external circumstances. An attempt has been made to achieve this in the study, described in Chapter 11, of the influences on the performance of small firms in instrumentation.

Breadth of product and customer group portfolios

The extent that it should specialize by type of product or customer is one of the key strategic decisions that must be faced by any small firm. A trade-off is likely between the reduction in risk from offering a broad range of products and the advantages from specialization. The latter can arise in many forms but clearly specialists are taking a gamble that either no adverse changes in market conditions will occur or that they will be able to cope with any such changes. Similarly, there are advantages from focusing on the needs of a particular group of customers, but such a strategy exposes small firms to a fall in demand occurring faster than it proves possible to diversify into a broader customer base.

Given the importance of this aspect of management it was covered in some detail. Questions were included on the number of product groups offered, the percentage of sales from the main product group, whether different products were sold to similar types of customers and the proportion of sales made to the main customer group.

Standardization

Whether only standard products were offered or whether they were tailor-made to suit the needs of individual customers. The former offers the opportunity to exploit economies of scale, the latter probably to charge premium prices. Some degree of economies of scale are almost inevitable though small firms will not normally prove successful at competing head-on with large firms in segments in which such economies are substantial. One possible route to circumventing the advantages from scale of output is to exploit those from 'learning by doing', which for small firms offers the distinct advantage that costs are not affected by how much is currently produced but how much has been produced in the past; hence, the phenomena of the long established, well respected and highly profitable small specialist whose scale of output would sometimes appear to defy the economic logic of their sector (see Chapter 8).

Subcontracting

Whether more than 50 per cent of sales came from subcontracting. Such a route will remove the need to market to the final customer but offers less scope for adding value.

Pricing policy

Whether the company attempted to achieve competitive advantage through lower prices or costs, treated as one variable, or through product quality, treated as a separate variable. The assumption was that low price strategies offer less room for strategic manoeuvre because they will usually only prove effective in markets characterized by low product differentiation. Moreover, even if the benefits from a low price strategy should be enjoyed in a significantly higher volume of sales, for SMEs the absolute increase in profits that accompanies this may prove insufficient to fund a significant increase in productive capacity.

Recent changes

Whether over the previous three years there had been an extension in the range of products offered, or customer groups served, treated as separate variables, or whether the domestic market had been expanded. The assumption was that growth would result from such dynamism.

Country

If it were possible to design a questionnaire that encompassed all of the influences on performance – a clearly impossible task – including the nationality of a firm would be superfluous. Whereas country-specific factors can take many forms, the set of attitudes, values and perceptions which collectively constitute the business culture, would be one example, the social economic environment, another, in a perfectly specified model which exactly measures the influences on performance, these would be reflected in the other variables, some internal to the firm, some external. In the absence of the ideal questionnaire, implied by such a model, it is appropriate to include nationality as a separate factor in order to compare the importance of aspects of management behaviour with which it is correlated – how hard managers are prepared to work, for instance, or their willingness to take risks or their creativity – but which are omitted from the study, with the importance of those factors included.

Industry

Similar considerations apply with respect to the effects of industry variables on growth. If all such variables could be included in a questionnaire there would be no need to include food, clothing/footwear or electronics as separate variables. But it would be difficult to design a questionnaire that would be that comprehensive. Not only would it need to encompass all the dimensions of market structure, and to do so in precisely the theoretically correct way, but also those of an industry's culture. Whereas economists traditionally have ignored either the existence of inter-sector differences in culture and whether any such differences might affect differences in performance, the validity of such positions can only be established empirically.

RESULTS

(Full regression results are shown in Tables 12.2 and 12.3.)

Table 12.1 shows the ranking[3] of the twenty-three variables that

Table 12.1 Ranking of importance of major influences on proportionate growth

---

High importance

---

1 Percentage of sales from main product group
2 if British
3 if French
4 if main product group generates sales throughout world (NEGATIVE)
5 if competitors are mainly 'big' (NEGATIVE)
6 if Finnish
7 if in clothing (NEGATIVE)
8 if offering a standard product (NEGATIVE)

Medium importance

---

9 Percentage of sales to main customer group
10 if business involves very complex technology
11 if in food
12 Number of customer groups (NEGATIVE)
13 if competitors are mainly very small to medium (NEGATIVE)
14 if market is 'large' or 'very large'

Low importance

---

15 if 'no importance' is attached to 'financial independence', 'doing better than other businesses' or 'a high level of income'
16 if over the last three years new products have been introduced
17 if over the last three years there has been an extension of the domestic market
18 if needs of customers are 'very differentiated'
19 if father was 'a civil servant, in business, retailing or was a professional'

Table 12.1   (continued)

20	if over the last three years there had been an extension of customer groups
21	if demand is 'fairly regular' (NEGATIVE)
22	if products linked by 'same customer needs or buying habits'

collectively had the greatest impact on the proportionate growth rates experienced by the SMEs in the samples included in the STRATOS study.

The conclusions that might be drawn from these results are:

- *Focus* The greatest proportionate growth was enjoyed by European SMEs that derived their sales from a single main product group. This is probably testimony to the importance to SMEs of not spreading their marketing effort too widely. The importance of focus is reinforced by the positive correlation between growth and the proportion of sales to the main customer group and the negative correlation with the number of customer groups. This would suggest that the advantages from a broad portfolio of customer groups – especially economies of scope – would not appear to outweigh those from concentrating on the needs of a particular group of customers. It should, however, be pointed out that in the absence of economies of scope, and if firms extend their customer groups (or products, or the markets in which they operate, the principle is the same) in decreasing order of performance, their risk and return will both fall. This implies that firms with a narrow customer (or product or market) base will be more likely either to do very well or to fail. Because the STRATOS study only included a cross-section of survivors – and it is hard to see how it could have done otherwise – it is not possible to estimate the failure rate among the more highly focused SMEs.

- *Export orientation* It is conceivable that similar consideration should govern the interpretation of the low rates of growth experienced by firms that earned their sales worldwide rather than concentrating on a particular market, whether domestic or foreign. A more likely explanation is that owners of firms that sold worldwide underestimated the problems of breaking into new overseas markets. Perhaps, also, firms were forced to look for sales wherever they could find them when they suffered from falling demand in the more established market with which they were familiar.

- *Standardization* Regardless of the apparent benefits to sales from focusing on a narrow range of products or customer groups the highest rates of growth were not enjoyed by the firms offering a standard product. The implied alternative of some degree of tailor-making to suit the needs of individual customers would appear to represent a more effective route to higher growth.

- *Size of competitors* Companies whose main competitors were described as 'big' experienced the lowest rates of growth. They may quite simply have been victims of economies of scale or scope but this begs the question of whether they had generally been operating in established markets in which circumstances had changed to their disadvantage or in new markets in which advantages from size had not previously been apparent. A clue to the answer is perhaps provided by the negative relationship between growth and whether competitors were described as 'very small to medium', though the relationship is not as strong as when competitors are big. The implication is that the highest rates of growth were experienced by firms, the size of whose competitors were described as 'a mixture' of sizes. Such a situation would be most likely in markets which offer the opportunities for performance levels sufficiently high to attract big firms but which are not characterized by economies of scale or, at least, the advantages not so obvious as to deter entry by small firms.

- *Nationality and sector* In spite of the comprehensiveness of the STRATOS questionnaire there would appear to remain significant nationality and sector specific factors that it did not encompass. It should be noted that these do not simply reflect differences in rates of growth between countries and sectors. Whereas the samples of SMEs located in the UK and Finland on average experienced an absolute growth in sales between 1980 and 1983 of 122.2 per cent and 50.4 per cent respectively, giving them first and second place in the performance league table, French companies on average achieved only 22.2 per cent, giving them seventh place. After taking into account the effects of all the other factors included in the study there were still some that were special to firms operating in the UK, Finland and France that made a positive contribution to their growth. Similarly, whereas European clothing and food SMEs on average achieved about the same absolute growth (26.2 per cent and 26.8 per cent respectively), the 'clothing factor' was negative, the 'food factor' positive, meaning that, taking into account the pro-portion of firms that benefited from various internal and external influences on performance, clothing firms should, on average, have achieved higher growth and food companies would have been expected to have done less well.

- *State of demand* Unless the food and clothing sector variables are picking up the effects of differences in market conditions, the latter do not appear to represent major influences on growth. Only the variable describing the size of the market achieved as much as a middle ranking in importance. A certain dynamism in conditions, whether external to the firm, or whether reflecting its strategic conditions, would appear to have been minor influences on performance: if new products had been introduced, or if there had been an extension in the size of the domestic market or in the number of customer groups. Perhaps it is part of the same pattern that companies whose owners described the demand for their products as being 'fairly regular' suffered the lowest rates of growth, though it must be emphasized that this relationship was very weak. This serves as confirmation of the low importance to performance of market conditions suggested in Chapter 11.

- *Characteristics of owners* The age of owners and the years of full-time education did not figure within the twenty most important influences on growth, though this does not imply that these variables make absolutely no difference. Other personal characteristics were shown to have some impact on growth, albeit very weak. It would appear that owners who claimed to attach a low priority to financial objectives on average achieved the higher rates of growth for their companies. By implication the most successful owners were more interested in benefits from running an expanding business such as self-fulfilment, or social status, or the security it might provide for their families. The owners from middle class backgrounds might also, on average, achieve higher rates of growth than those whose backgrounds were more modest. In the UK, in which the social class into which an individual is born is arguably the single most important influence on his or her lifetime earnings (and, indeed, on many other dimensions on which personal success is normally measured), this relationship is, perhaps, not surprising, but it would appear to be a Europe-wide phenomenon.

- *Technology* Companies, on average, enjoyed higher rates of growth if their businesses were described as involving 'very complex technology'. Several explanations are possible for this relationship, albeit that it is only weak. It may be that the most advanced technology is associated with new, dynamic markets, for instance, or that the companies that acknowledge the importance of technology are the most likely to be successful.

- *Customer differentiation* Markets can be differentiated with respect to products or to customers, though attempting to satisfy differing customer needs would imply a differentiation in products. Markets that are highly differentiated offer the most scope for competing on non-price dimensions and for exhibiting creativity in strategic management. What is surprising is the low ranking that this variable achieved, though the importance of product differentiation may, to some extent, have been picked up by the importance of not offering a standard product.
- *Similar customer needs* This presumably reflects a type of economy of scale.

CONCLUDING REMARKS

The STRATOS project was an ambitious study and the database it generated will continue to be a valuable source of information on European SMEs. As far as conclusions about the reasons for growth are concerned some were strongly country and sector specific. Identifying precisely what these might be must await further research.

The clear message from these results is that firms exhibiting the highest rates of growth have been those that were highly focused in their marketing towards a single product group and avoided spreading their efforts too widely throughout the world. The former was suggested by the instrumentation study. On the other hand, the importance of supplying quality, suggested by the latter, was not confirmed by STRATOS, though there was some implication of this from the negative relationship with the supply of standardised products. Both studies point to the inadvisability of competing in markets dominated by bigger companies, though possibly the highest growth rates are achieved in markets in which the benefits, if any of size, have not yet been realized.

APPENDIX I

Table 12.2 Influences on growth

Proportionate growth	=	0.326 (X_1),	+	0.395 (X_2),	+	0.425 (X_3),	
		(5.1)		(6.3)		(7.4)	
	−	0.203 (X_4),	+	0.152 (X_5),	+	0.125 (X_6)	
		(−3.3)		(2.3)		(3.7)	
	−	0.129 (X_7),	−	0.294 (X_8),	−	0.667 (X_9)	
		(−1.5)		(−3.3)		(−5.6)	
	−	1.134 (X_{10}),	−	0.0021 (X_{11}),	+	0.0058 (X_{12})	
		(−5.9)		(−4.2)		(3.6)	
	+	0.164 (X_{13}),	+	0.301 (X_{14}),	+	0.147 (X_{15})	
		(1.6)		(3.1)		(1.97)	
	+	0.355 (X_{16}),	+	0.0129 (X_{17}),	−	0.138 (X_{18})	
		(2.9)		(6.9)		(−1.5)	
	−	0.383 (X_{19}),	+	0.205 (X_{20}),	+	0.246 (X_{21})	
		(−3.8)		(2.0)		(2.2)	
	+	0.849 (X_{22}),	−	0.817 (X_{23})			
		(2.04)		(−3.3)			

$\overline{R}^2 = 0.74$ SEE = 0.14 Degrees of freedom = 71 F = 13.072 ('t' statistics shown in brackets)

X_1 = if Finnish
X_2 = if French
X_3 = if British
X_4 = if in clothing
X_5 = if in food
X_6 = if the market is large or very large
X_7 = if demand is fairly regular
X_8 = if competitors are mainly 'very small' to 'medium'
X_9 = if competitors are mainly 'big'
X_{10} = if main product group generates sales throughout the world
X_{11} = number of customer groups
X_{12} = percentage of sales to the main customer group
X_{13} = if needs of customers are very differentiated
X_{14} = if business involves very complex technology
X_{15} = if father's occupation was a 'civil servant, in business, retailing or was a professional'
X_{16} = if 'no importance' is attached to 'financial independence', 'doing better than other businessmen' or 'high level of income'
X_{17} = percentage of sales from main product group
X_{18} = if product linked by same 'customers needs or buying habits'
X_{19} = if 'customer offered a standard product'
X_{20} = if over the last three years new products had been offered
X_{21} = over the last three years there had been an extension of the domestic market
X_{22} = over the last three years there had been an extension of customer groups
X_{23} = constant

Table 12.3 Standardized coefficients in descending order of magnitude

X_{17}	0.509
X_3	0.505
X_2	0.43
X_{10}	-0.407
X_9	-0.391
X_1	0.387
X_4	-0.340
X_{19}	-0.312
X_{12}	0.291
X_{14}	0.263
X_5	0.256
X_{11}	-0.253
X_8	-0.246
X_6	0.222
X_{16}	0.190
X_{20}	0.154
X_{21}	0.147
X_{13}	0.134
X_{15}	0.132
X_{22}	0.120
X_7	-0.116
X_{18}	-0.101

13

POLICY IMPLICATIONS

This book has avoided any discussion of the effects of government policy on the performance of small firms or of the equally contentious question of whether their performance is detrimented by inefficiencies in the capital market.[1] To a limited extent some of the findings it reports do have implications for the latter question. Surely the undercapitalization that was so frequently blamed by the victims of compulsory liquidation cannot simply be dismissed as a convenient scapegoat. Nor can it be totally without interest that the most profitable within the sample of instrumentation companies were those reporting the biggest shortfall between the amount they requested from their banks and the amount they received, though this would not appear to represent evidence that their success had been constrained by the parsimony displayed by banks.

Although the primary purpose of this book is to aid the policies pursued by decision-makers within small firms, its conclusions, however, may have implications for public policy, if this were to involve the establishment of some sort of nationally controlled development bank. It should be emphasized that adopting such a policy need not imply criticism of conventional banks, only that there is a need for a particular kind of institution within the capital market which is unlikely to be satisfied by the commercial sector.

A development bank could have any of a number of roles:

- It could serve as an instrument of a national industrial strategy to attempt to redress the chronic structural weaknesses within the British economy. This would involve targeting specific industries for funds to encourage the expansion of existing firms and establishment of new. Such a strategy would recognize that to claim that 'the government cannot pick winners' demonstrates a peculiarly

Anglo-Saxon view not shared by many other countries that are avowedly capitalist.

- A development bank could put more emphasis on long-term and closer relationships with its customers than is commonly the case with conventional banks. This could mean supplying a greater proportion of long-term loans, more detailed and regular advice and possibly even taking an equity stake. Additionally it could serve as an agency to match owners of small firms with private sources of capital, now fashionably termed 'business angels'.[2] Certainly some attempt should be made to plug the equity gap that so obviously exists and has been identified in a succession of government sponsored reports.[3] The degree that any scheme for injecting fresh equity into their companies would be attractive to owners must remain an open question. Repayment schedules for loans reduce flexibility in the management of cashflow but are not supposed to result in the dilution of autonomy usually assumed to accompany the sharing of ownership, though the actual trade-off would depend upon the conditions imposed when granting a loan compared to the extent that the new joint owners would expect to play a part in the running of the company. But what is being suggested would only be an addition to existing banking services. It is hard to see the disadvantages from an extension of choice.

- A development bank could adopt employment generation as one of its objectives. Arguably concentrations within communities of long-term unemployment will erode the work ethic that serves as the most effective antidote to the welfare trap, i.e. the disincentive to work produced by a narrow margin between low pay and welfare payments. A real danger exists that if the habit of work is lost, the ending of the current recession would not lead to opportunities to gain employment being taken by many within what is sometimes labelled the 'underclass'. Unemployment is also associated with some categories of crime and with some forms of ill-health. Subsidies to companies to increase the size of their workforces could, therefore, prove cost-effective, though actually carrying out the cost–benefit exercise would be a formidable endeavour.

On a rather narrower criteria, subsidies might also pay their way if it could be shown that specific people were never likely to work again, so that subsidies were not interfering with the optimum allocation of resources. Any subsidy below the cost to the taxpayer of their being unemployed (consisting of welfare payments and foregone taxes) would actually save money.

The relevance to a development bank of the conclusions to be drawn from preceeding chapters is that, whatever its role, great care would need to be exercised in deciding which companies should be recipients of its funds. There is undoubtedly some truth in the frequently cited defence of the practices adopted by conventional banks, that these are a reaction to the high failure rate within the small-firm sector.[4] 'In order to avoid a development bank suffering an inconceivably high incidence of bad investment within its portfolio, it would prove essential to vet carefully applicants for its funds and to make attendance on a training course a condition for receiving an investment. The factors associated with the probability of survival, and with the likely performance among survivors, would obviously be taken into account in both the vetting of applicants and in the syllabuses of their training courses.

Some of the more important conclusions to be drawn by a development bank, teachers of small firm management and, not least, the owners of small firms themselves would be:

- *Market structure* For firms of all sizes the structure of the markets in which they operate could have an impact on the performance of small firms, though it has been argued that it may prove more helpful to think in terms of the markets for the characteristics constituting products, rather than treating products as homogeneous. Where small firms may differ from large is in the extent of their vulnerability to the structural forces by which they will be buffeted. By definition they will be limited in their capacity for exploiting economies of scale and so are denied the protection of perhaps the most important barrier to entry. Small firms that will prove most successful can create or exploit other forms of barriers, those created by knowledge being the most obvious. In some sectors buyer power will be so strong as to raise the question of whether they can truly be regarded as independent. If feasible, such firms should try to spread their customer base. Similar diversification will not be possible for anyone confronted with a tight franchise agreement. Such an agreement may make excellent financial sense for potential franchisees but they would be well advised to consider how far the agreement will leave them with the freedom normally resulting from running one's own business.

The evidence from the empirical studies reported here is a little mixed on the size of competitors which is most disadvantageous to the performance of small firms. Members of the sample of instrumentation companies that competed primarily with larger firms suffered the lowest rates of growth and profitability. Facing mostly larger firms also represented one of the most important negative influences on the growth displayed by firms included in the STRATOS study. This pleasing consistency is a little marred by the lower growth rates experienced by firms competing mainly with other SMEs. The most likely explanation is that the third possible category, where competitors were drawn from a mixture of size ranges, probably were found in unstable markets in which the advantages from size had not as yet been realized or if there were no such advantages, their markets had not so far become overcrowded with small companies. For firms fortunate enough to have a choice such markets would appear to offer the most attractive possibilities for growth.

- *Strategy* The results from the instrumentation and STRATOS studies may be regarded as complimentary. In the former the highest returns on sales and rates of growth were earned by companies with a clear view of their likely customers which aimed to provide high quality products. In the STRATOS sample there was a very high correlation between growth and the percentage of sales from the main product group, and a reasonably high correlation with the percentage of sales to the main customer group. It would seem that growth is most readily achieved by focusing marketing effort, on a narrow range of product groups and a narrow group of customers. This message is reinforced by the negative effect of spreading marketing effort througout the world, again suggesting the advisability of concentrating one's exporting efforts.
- *Human capital* The benefits to the performance of small firms from the education of their owners was not as strong as might be expected. Owners in the sample of construction companies with low levels of education certainly were more vulnerable to failure than those with HNDs or equivalent but the three owners with degrees also saw their firms fail. This hint of a U-shaped relationship is slightly strengthened when the relationship between different levels of education and growth in the instrumentation sector are considered in isolation from that of other variables, rather than in the stepwise procedure which did not identify any of the measures as relatively very important. Owners with degrees achieved higher rates of growth than those with HNDs or PhDs.

However, the picture is muddled by the results of applying the stepwise procedure to the possible influences on the profitability of instrumentation companies. The possession of an HND was pinpointed as an important variable, implying a negative relationship between education levels and profitability, though it should be remembered that none in the sample was uneducated.

Although it would be almost inconceivable if the volume of human capital within a small firm did not make a positive difference to its performance it would not seem that simple education levels of owners is a particularly appropriate measure. It is, perhaps, not without significance that in the STRATOS study the age of owners, the number of years of their full-time education, or whether they had attended a management course, were not identified as in the twenty-two most important influences on growth.

It is possible to be rather more categorical about forms of human capital other than that embodied in owners of small firms. Employing a skilled workforce was positively correlated with the growth of instrumentation companies and the probability of survival of the firms in the construction sector. The latter was also related to the willingness to take advice from external experts, which represents a route for supplementing the volume of human capital within a firm.

- *Management of cashflow* The negative relationship between the time taken to pay bills and both the probability of survival in the construction sector and the likely return on sales within instrumentation was a little surprising, given the obvious advantages from late payment, as was the strength of the relationships. It would be tempting to conclude that paying bills early would, in itself, lead to enhanced performance, perhaps from the resulting goodwill among suppliers. This might be a little rash, considering that prompt payment may be merely a symptom of an all round efficiency. On the other hand, whether a cause or symptom, the relationship might be useful in assessing credit worthiness by the capital market. The relationship would seem robust and the variable easy to measure, which is all that can be asked by an assessor in a commercial or development bank or a venture capitalist.

CONCLUDING REMARKS

This book has invited the reader to peer into the murky waters in which small firms may be found swimming. There are some suggestions as to what life in their pond is like, why some survive into old age, whilst others perish early, and if why some appear to prosper others merely get by.

Future research will continue the process of clarifying the water.

If nothing else, the message from previous pages is that studying the small firm sector is interesting and important and should not be consigned to an academic ghetto.

NOTES

2 PERFORMANCE, SIZE AND AGE

1 This is an inference from the apparent positive relationship between firm size and directors' remuneration in the quoted sector, though it is conceivable that the relationship may not be maintained when extrapolated into the small-firm sector. It should also be noted that there is not complete consensus about the existence of this relationship in even the quoted sector (Roberts, 1959; McGuire, Chin and Elbing, 1962; Lewellan and Huntsman, 1970; Yarrow, 1972; Ciscel and Carroll, 1980; Smyth, Boyles and Peseau, 1975; Cosh, 1975; Meeks and Whittington, 1975).

3 WHICH SMALL FIRMS FAIL?

1 These had not at this juncture failed, but, given the tone and title (*The Failure Syndrome*) of the paper it would not seem inappropriate to include it in this review.
2 It should be emphasized that Bates' (1990) methodology is above reproach.
3 Defined as negative net present value.
4 Which will be defined in the next chapter.

4 WHAT OFFICIAL RECEIVERS' REPORTS REVEAL ABOUT FAILURE

1 For a full description of the study on which this chapter is based refer to Hall and Young (1991) and Hall (1992).
2 Throughout this chapter statistical significance is defined as the rejection of the hypothesis of no difference at 0.05 per cent on an x^2 distribution.

3   If the population divided equally between two categories, A and B, and all As were geniuses and all Bs morons, the contingency table would be:

	A	B
genius	100	0
	(50)	(50)
moron	0	100
	(50)	(50)

and would be depicted in this chapter as:

	A	B
genius	+	–
moron	–	+

4   This hypothesis would be rejected at practically all levels of significance on an x^2 distribution.
5   'Bad' implying a difference between observed and expected of, at least, +5 and 'good' of, at least, –5.
6   There are too many cells with an expected value of less than five to safely allow the assumption of an x^2 distribution.

5   WHICH FIRMS FAIL: THE CASE OF CONSTRUCTION

1   The results of this study have already been reported in Hall (1994).
2   These were conducted by Roland Ashley, Mark Frost, John McClusker, Julian Mellantin, Agnes Nairn, David Nuttall and Konrad Urbanski, and processed by Panos Louroudjiatis, all of whom were participants on Manchester Business Schools, MBA programme.
3   NHBS Year Book, Kompass database, Fame database, Building Employers Confederation - North West Region Directory, telephone directories.
4   References provided in the concluding chapter.

6   THE PERFORMANCE OF SMALL FIRMS AND OWNER CHARACTERISTICS

1   A rigorous discussion is provided by Gibb and Scott (1983).
2   Bamberger (1983) provides an excellent review of methodology.
3   Chell, Haworth and Brearley (1991) and Hébert and Link (1988) provide excellent reviews.
4   Brockhaus (1980) cleverly argues that a strong desire to avoid failure may lead to entrepreneurs pursuing strategies that are either very safe or very risky, the latter because they cannot be blamed for their failure. His survey of a sample of the recently self-employed and samples of managers employed in companies did not suggest any differences in risk-preference.
5   See Stanworth, Blyth, Granger and Stanworth (1989) for a review.

7 STRATEGIC PLANNING AND THE SMALL FIRM

1 He has produced a dauntingly long stream of seminal papers on this and related topics, which includes Mintzberg (1978, 1990); Mintzberg and Waters (1982, 1985); Mintzberg and McHugh (1985) and Mintzberg, Brunet and Waters (1986).

2 This would appear to be contrary to the view of the eminent forecaster, Armstrong (1982), who argued that formal planning has more value in the presence of high levels of uncertainty and complexity.

9 MARKET STRUCTURE

1 Though valient attempts have been made by modern proponents of game theory.

2 Cunningham (1980) provides the best description.

3 Hakansson (1982) and Wilson, Hansang-Lin and Holler (1989) are useful starting points.

4 Many of the points made here are drawn from the definitive textbook on small-firm financial management written by McMahon, Holmes, Hutchinson and Forsaith (1993).

10 ORGANIZATION LIFECYCLES

1 Mueller's (1972) lifecycle theory is useful in explaining the behaviour of quoted companies.

2 See also Miller and Toulouse (1986).

3 The reader may judge that the authors were anticipating this criticism when they attached the rather puzzling footnote, 'Where these criteria are used to classify our periods into phases, they were never used to compare them or to test the hypothesis'.

4 The author gives the mean values of the companies' ages, sales growth and employment size at each stage, pointing out the correlation between them but is not entirely clear how companies were allocated that did not conform to this pattern, for instance, old firms with a continuing high rate of growth.

11 THE RELATIVE IMPORTANCE OF INFLUENCES ON PERFORMANCE

1 Multitudinous thanks are extended to Gail Adams for timelessly and ingeniously carrying out the econometrics for this study. Sally Fulshaw collected the data.

2 See Gibb and Scott (1985) for a comprehensive list of likely possibilities. Among those that have not been included in earlier discussions are the benefits to small firms from employing outside consultants (Robinson, 1982) and from maintaining external contracts or 'boundary spanning' (Dollinger, 1984).

3 In regression this would be the distinction between high-valued 't' statistics and high-valued coefficients.

4 Vesper (1990) provides a useful survey of the literature, as well as case material, on factors associated with the performance of new ventures.

5 The strength of this assertion is somewhat surprising given the authors' concession regarding the weakness of using non-parametric statistics: 'we could not measure the magnitude of our statistical relationships. Thus it was difficult to compare the effects of two different variables in terms of their bottom-line impact'.

6 As measured by the minimalization of Mallow's Cp.

7 As spelt out by Lovell (1983) though useful contributions on this have been made by Ames and Reiter (1961) and Mayer (1975) with the antecedence to some of their points being traced to Orcutt (1948).

8 This represents one of the most comprehensive databases available to researchers on strategy. A recent guide to the results of some of the studies that have been based on it is provided by Buzzell and Gale (1987).

9 Their own empirical study (Sandberg and Hofer, 1987) implied that industry concentration was included in the list of explanatory variables but no mention was made in their list of statistically significant relationships.

12 INFLUENCES ON GROWTH: AN INTERNATIONAL COMPARISON

1 This is fully reported in Adams and Hall (1994).

2 The other members of the team were Rik Donckels, Erwin Frohlich, Eduard Gabele, Antti Haahti, Klaus Haake, Kees Koning, Allan Lehtimaki, Hans Pichler, Jan van der Wilde and Alastair Weir.

3 Relative importance was established be comparing the size of standardized coefficients, derived by multiplying each regression coefficient by the ratio of the standard deviation of the relevant variable to the standard deviation of the growth rates.

13 POLICY IMPLICATIONS

1 Banking practices towards small firms are considered by Berry *et al.* (1993a, 1993b, 1993c); Binks, Ennew and Reed (1990); Binks and Ennew (1994); Ennew and Binks (1993a, 1993b); Deakins and Hussain (1991) and Deakins, Hussain and Ram (1992). The attitudes of their customers by the Federation of Small Businesses (1993); and Forum of Private Businesses (1993); Binks, Ennew and Reed (1990). International comparisons of bank–customer relations are provided by Binks, Ennew and Reed (1992); Deakins and Philpott (1993) and 3i Cranfield European Business Centre (1993). A sympathetic view of current banking practices is supplied by Cressey (1993); Keasey and Watson (1992) and Storey (1993).

2 The term is usually associated with Wetzel (1986a, 1986b). For a thorough discussion of the British informal venture capital market, and of the

possible role of business angels, see Harrison and Mason (1992, 1993a, 1993b); Mason and Harrison (1989, 1992, 1993) and Mason, Harrison and Challoner (1991).

3 Macmillan (1931); Wilson (1974).
4 The culture within the banking sector must also play a part. The practices and attitudes adopted by British banks are not necessarily matched by banks in other countries.

BIBLIOGRAPHY

Ackelsberg, R. and Arlow, P. (1985) 'Small businesses do plan and it pays off', *Long Range Planning*, **18**, 5, 61–67.

Altman, E.I. (1968) 'Financial ratios, discriminant analysis and the prediction of corporate bankruptcy', *Journal of Finance*, **23**, 4, 589–609.

—— (1984) 'The success of business failure prediction models: an international survey', *Journal of Banking and Finance*, **8**, 1, 171–198.

Ames, E. and Reiter, S. (1961) 'Distributions of correlation coefficients in economic time series', *Journal of the American Statistical Association*, **56**, 637–656.

Argenti, J. (1976) *Corporate Collapse, The Causes and Symptoms*, London: McGraw Hill.

—— (1985) 'Corporate Planning', *Accountants Digest* Spring/70, 1–12.

Armstrong, S.J. (1982) 'The value of formal planning for strategic decisions, review of empirical research', *Strategic Management Journal*, **3**, 197–211.

Bamberger, I. (1983) 'Value systems, strategies and the performance of small and medium sized firms', *European Small Business Journal*, **1**, 4, 25–39.

Bannock, G. and Morgan, V.E. (1988) *Banks and Small Business: An International Perspective*, A report prepared for the Forum of Private Business and the National Federation of Independent Business.

Bates, T. (1990) 'Entrepreneur human capital inputs and small business longevity', *Review of Economics and Statistics*, **72**, 4, 551–559.

Beaver, W.H. (1967) 'Financial ratios as predictors of failure', *The Journal of Accounting Research*, **5**, 71–111.

—— (1968) 'Alternative accounting measures as predictors of failure', *The Accounting Review*, 42, 113–122.

Begley, T.M. and Boyd, D.P. (1986) 'Executive and corporate correlates of financial performance in smaller firms', *Journal of Small Business Management*, **24**, 2, 8–14.

—— (1987) 'Psychological characteristics associated with performance in entrepreneurial firms and smaller businesses', *Journal of Business Venturing*, **2**, 79–93.

Berry, A., Faulkner, S., Hughes, M. and Jarvis, R. (1993a) 'The use of forecasts by banks: the case of small business lending', *University of Brighton, Department of Finance and Accounting Occasional Paper Series, Number 23*.

—— (1993b) 'The role of bankers' visits to clients in UK small business lending', *University of Brighton, Department of Finance and Accounting Occasional Paper Series, Number 22.*

—— (1993c) 'Financial information, the banker and the small business', *British Accounting Review,* **25,** 131–150.

Berryman, J. (1983) 'Small business failure and bankruptcy: a survey of the literature', *European Small Business Journal,* **1,** 4, 47–59.

Biggadike, R.E. (1979) *Corporate Diversification: Entry Strategy and Performance,* Boston: Harvard University.

Binks, M.R. and Ennew, C.T. (1994) 'Bank finance for growing small businesses', in Buckland, R., and Davis, E.W. (eds) *Finance in Growing Firms,* London: Routledge.

Binks, M.R., Ennew, C.T. and Reed, G.V. (1990) 'Assymetric information and the banks/small firm relationship in the UK', Department of Economics, University of Nottingham, Discussion Paper No 90/1.

—— (1992) 'Small businesses and their banks: an international perspective', National Westminster Bank through Nottingham University Consultants.

Birley, S. and Westhead, P. (1990) 'The growth and performance contrasts between "types" of small firms', *Strategic Management Journal,* **2,** 535–557.

Blum, M. (1974) 'Failing company discriminant analysis', *Journal of Accounting Research,* **12,** 1, 1–26.

Bolton Committee (1971) *Report of the Committee of Enquiry into Small Firms* (CMND 4811). London: HMSO.

Boston Consulting Group (1970) *Perspectives on Experience,* Boston: BCG.

Bracker, J.S. and Pearson, J.N. (1985) 'The impact of consultants on small firm strategic planning' *Journal of Small Business Management,* **23,** 3, 23–30.

Bracker, J., Keats, B.W. and Pearson, J.N. (1986) 'Planning and financial planning of small mature firms', *Strategic Management Journal,* **7,** 503–522.

—— (1988) 'Planning and financial performance among small firms in a growth industry' *Strategic Management Journal,* **9,** 591–603.

Bradburd, R.M. and Ross, D.R. (1989) 'Can small firms find and defend strategic niches? A test of the Porter hypothesis', *The Review of Economics and Statistics,* **71,** 258–262.

Brockhaus, R.H. Snr (1980) 'Risk taking propensity of entrepreneurs', *Academy of Management Journal,* **23,** 3, 509–520.

Brooksbank, R., Kirby, D.A. and Wright, G. (1992) 'Marketing and company performance: an examination of medium sized manufacturing firms in Britain', *Small Business Economics,* **4,** 3, 221–236.

Bulow, J.I. and Shoven, J.B. (1978) 'The bankruptcy decision', *The Bell Journal of Economics,* **9,** 437–456.

Campbell, A. (1991) 'Brief case: strategy and intuition – a conversation with Henry Mintzberg', *Long Range Planning,* **24,** 2, 108–110.

Campbell, N.C.G. (1985) 'An interaction approach to organizational buying behaviour', *Journal of Business Research,* **13,** 35–45.

Carland, J.W., Carland, J.C. and Carroll, D.A., Jnr (1989) 'An assessment of the psychological determinants of planning in small businesses', *International Small Business Journal*, 7, 4, 23–34.

Carr, C.H. and Truesdale, (1992) 'Lessons from Nisson's British suppliers' *International Journal of Operations and Production Management*, 12, 2, 49–57.

Casey, C.J., Jnr (1980) 'The usefulness of accounting ratios for subjects' predictions of corporate failure: replication and extensions' *Journal of Accounting Research*, 18, 2, 603–613.

Chaganti, R. (1987) 'Small business strategies in different industry growth environments', *Journal of Small Business Management*, July, 61–68.

Chaganti, R., Chaganti, R. and Mahajan, V. (1989) 'Profitable, small business strategies under difficult kinds of competition', *Entrepreneurship: Theory and Practice*, Spring, 21–35.

Chandler, A.D., Jnr (1962) *Strategy and Structure: Chapters in the History of the Industrial Enterprise*, Cambridge: MIT Press.

Channon, D.F. (1973) *Strategy and Structure of British Enterprise*, London: Macmillan.

Chrisman, J.J. and Leslie, J. (1989) 'Strategic, administrative and operating problems: the impact of outsiders on small firm performance', *Entrepreneurship: Theory and Practice*, Spring, 37–51.

Churchill, N.C. and Lewis, V.L. (1983) 'The five stages of small business growth', *Harvard Business Review*, May–June, 30–50.

Ciscel, D.H. and Carroll, T. (1980) 'The determinants of executive salaries', *Review of Economics and Statistics*, 67, 171–174.

Coase, R.H. (1937) 'The nature of the firm', *Economica*, 4, 386–405.

Cooper, A.C. (1985) 'The role of incubator organizations in the founding of growth oriented firms', *Journal of Business Venturing*, 1, 75–86.

Cosh, A. (1975) 'The Remuneration of chief executives in the United Kingdom', *Economic Journal*, 85, 75–94.

Covin, J.G. and Slevin, D.P. (1989) 'Strategic management of small firms in hostile and benign environments', *Strategic Management Journal*, 10, 1, 75–87.

Cragg, P.B. and King, M. (1988) 'Organizational characteristics and small firms' performance revisited', *Entrepreneurship: Theory and Practice*, 13, 2, 49–64.

Cressey, R. (1993), 'Business borrowing and control: a theory of entrepreneurial types', *SME Centre Warwick Business School Working Paper*.

Cressey, R. (1993), 'Loan commitments and business starts: an empirical investigation on UK data', *SME Centre, Warwick Business School Discussion Paper*.

Cunningham, M.T. (1980) 'International marketing and purchasing of industrial goods: features of a European research project', *European Journal of Marketing*, 14, 5/6, 322–338.

Cunningham, M.T. (1993) 'The power game: a study of power within supplier–customer relationships', Paper presented at 9th IMP Conference, University of Bath.

Cunningham, M.T. and Homse, E. (1986) 'Controlling the marketing-purchasing interface resource development and organizational implications', *Industrial Marketing and Purchasing*, 1, 2, 2–27.

Curran, J. and Blackburn, R. (1994) *Small Firms and Local Economic Networks – the Death of the Local Economy*, London: Chapman.

Cyert, R.M. and March, J.G. (1963) *A Behaviourial Theory of the Firm*, London: Prentice Hall.

Daly, M. (1991) 'VAT registration and deregistration in 1990', *Employment Gazette*, November, 579–582.

Deakin, E.B. (1977) 'Business failure prediction: an empirical analysis, in E.I. Altman and A.W. Sametz (eds) *Financial Crisis, Institutions and Markets in a Fragile Environment*, New York: Wiley.

Deakins, D. and Hussain, G. (1991) 'Risk assessment by bank managers', *University of Central England Working Paper*.

Deakins, D. and Philpott, (1993) 'Comparative European practices in the finance of small firms: UK Holland and Germany'.

Deakins, D., Hussain, G. and Ram, M. (1992) 'Finance of ethnic minority small business: a study of the finance of ethnic minority small firms in the West Midlands', *University of Central England Working Paper*.

Deshpande, R. and Parasuvaman, A. (1986) 'Linking corporate culture to strategic planning', *Business Horizons*, May–June, 28–37.

Dollinger, M.J. (1984) 'Environmental boundary spanning and information processing effects on organizational performance', *Academy of Management Journal*, 84, 2, 351–368.

Doukas, J. (1986) 'Bankers versus bankruptcy prediction models: an empirical investigation, 1979–82', *Applied Economics*, 18, 5, 479–493.

Drazin, R. and Kazanjian, R.K. (1990) 'A re-analysis of Miller and Friesen's lifecycle data', *Strategic Management Journal*, 11, 319–325.

Dunkelberg, W.C. and Cooper, A.C. (1982) 'Entrepreneurial typologies: an empirical study', in K.H. Vesper (ed.) *Frontiers of Entrepreneurial Research*, Wellesley, Mass: Boston College.

Dunne, T., Roberts, M.J. and Samuelson, L. (1988) 'Patterns of firm entry and exit in US manufacturing industries', *Rand Journal of Economics*, 19, 4, 495–515.

—— (1989) 'The growth and failure of US manufacturing plants', *Quarterly Journal of Economics*, 104, 4, 671–698.

Dyke, L.S., Fischer, E.M. and Reuber, R.A. (1992) 'An inter-industry examination of the impact of owner experience on firm performance', *Journal of Small Business Management*, October, 72–97.

Edmister, R.O. (1972) 'An empirical test of financial ratio analysis for small business failure prediction', *Journal of Financial and Quantitative Analysis*, 7, 1471–1493.

Ennew, C.T. and Binks, R. (1993a) 'The provisions of finance to small businesses: does the banking relationship constrain performance?', School of Management and Finance Discussion Paper, University of Nottingham, XIV.

——(1993b) 'Regional financial segmentation: small businesses and their banks in England and Scotland', XVII.

Evans, D.S. (1987a) 'The relationship between firm growth, size and age: estimates for 100 manufacturing industries', *Journal of Industrial Economics*, 35, 4, 567–582.

—— (1987b), 'Tests of alternative theories of firm growth', *Journal of Political Economy*, **45**, 4, 657–674.

Federation of Small Businesses (1993) 'A blue print for enterprise', *Policy Document from the Federation of Small Businesses*.

Felgner, B.H. (1989) 'Retailers grab power, control market place', *Marketing News*, **23**, 2, 1–2.

Filley, A.C. and Aldag, R.J. (1978) 'Characteristics and measurement of an organizational typology', *Academy of Management Journal*, **21**, 4, 578–591.

Ford, D. (1980) 'The development of buyer and seller relationships in industrial markets', *European Journal of Marketing*, **14**, 5, 339–354.

Forum of Private Businesses (1993a) 'Overdue payment of commercial debt: the UK national business disease', *Report by Forum of Private Businesses*.

Frey Sherwood, C. and Schlosser, M. (1993) 'ABB and Ford: creating value through co-operation', *Sloan Management Review*, **35**, 1, 65–72.

Ganguly, P. (1985) *UK Small Business Statistics and International Comparisons*, London: Harper & Row.

Gibb, A. and Scott, M. (1983) 'Strategic awareness, personal commitments and the process of planning in the small business', *Journal of Management Studies*, **22**, 6, 597–631.

Gibb, A. and Davies, L. (1990) 'In pursuit of frameworks for the development of growth models of the small business', *International Small Business Journal*, **9**,1, 15–31.

Greiner, L.E. (1972) 'Evolution and revolution as organizations grow', *Harvard Business Review*, July-Aug, 37–46.

Hakansson, H. (1982) *International Marketing and Purchasing of Industrial Goods*, London: J. Wiley.

Hall, G. (1989) 'Financial barriers to growth', in *Barriers to Growth*, J. Barber, J.S. Metcalfe and M. Porteous (eds), London: Croom Helm.

—— (1992) 'Reasons for insolvency amongst small firms – a review and fresh evidence', *Small Business Economics*, **4**, 237–250.

Hall, G. and Fulshaw, S. (1993) '*Success in the instrumentation sector*', in *Entrepreneurship and Business Development*, H. Klandt (ed.): Avebury.

Hall, G. and Howell, S. (1985) 'The experience curve from the economist's perspective', *Strategic Management Journal*, **6**, 3, 197–213.

Hall, G. and Young, B. (1991) 'Factors associated with insolvency amongst small firms', *International Small Business Journal*, **9**, 2, 54–63.

Hamer, M.M. (1983) 'Failure prediction: sensitivity of classification accuracy to alternative statistical methods and variable sets', *Journal of Accounting and Public Policy*, **2**, 4, 289–307.

Hand, J.H., Lloyd, W.P. and Rogow, R.B. (1982) 'Agency relationships in the close corporation', *Financial Management*, **11**, 1, 25–30.

Harrison, R.T. and Mason, C. (1992) 'International perspectives on the supply of informal venture capital', *Journal of Business Venturing*, **7**, 459–475.

—— (1993) 'Finance for the growing business: the role of informal investment', *National Westminster Quarterly Review*, May, 17–29.

Hartigan, P. (1976) 'Why companies fail', *Certified Accountant*, Dec, 400–402.

Hébert, R.F. and Link, A.N. (1988) *The Entrepreneur – Mainstream Views and Radical Critiques* (second edition), New York: Praeger.

Henderson, B. (1974) *The Experience Curve Reviewed III – How Does it Work?* Boston: BCG.

Hitchens, D.M.W.N. and O'Farrell, P.N. (1988) 'Comparative performance of small manufacturing companies in South Wales and Northern Ireland', *Omega*, 16, 5, 429–438.

Hobson, E.L. and Morrison, R.M. (1983) 'How do corporate start-up ventures fare?', in *Frontiers of Entrepreneurship*, Wellesley: Boston College.

Hofer, C.W. and Sandberg, W.R. (1987) 'Improving new venture performance: some guidelines for success', *American Journal of Small Business*, 12, 1, 11–25.

Hornaday, J.A. and Aboud, J. (1971) 'Characteristics of successful entrepreneurs', *Personnel Psychology*, 24, 2, 141–153.

Hornaday, R.W. and Wheatley, W.J. (1986) 'Managerial characteristics and the financial performance of small business', *Journal of Small Business Management*, 24, 2, 1–7.

Hudson, J. (1987), 'The age, regional and industrial structure of company liquidations', *Journal of Business Finance and Accounting*, 14, 2, 199–213.

Hutchinson, P.J. (1991) *Issues in Small Business Finance and Accounting, Working Paper No. 91–6, Department of Accounting and Financial Management, The University of New England, Armidale, New South Wales.*

Ibrahim, A.B. and Goodwin (1986) 'Perceived causes of success in small business', *American Journal of Small Business*, 2, 2, 41–49.

IMP 5th Conference. Institute for the Study of Business Markets: The Pennsylvania State University.

Jensen, M.C. and Meckling, W.H. (1976) 'Theory of the firm: managerial behaviour, agency costs and ownership structure', *Journal of Financial Economics*, 3, 4, 305–360.

Johns, B.L., Dunlop, W.C. and Sheehan, W.J. (1989) *Small Business in Australia*, Sydney: George Allen and Unwin.

Jovanovic, B. (1982) 'Selection and the evolution of industry', *Econometrica*, 50, 3, 649–670.

Kamal, S. and Hughety, K.J. (1977) 'Managerial problems of the small firms', *Journal of Small Business Management*, 15, 1, 37–42.

Kazanjian, R.K. (1988) 'Operationalising stage of growth: An empirical assessment of dominant problems' in J.A. Hornaday, F. Tarpley, J.A. Timmons and K.H. Vesper (eds) *Frontiers of Entrepreneurial Research*, Wellesley, Mass.: Babason College.

Keasey, K. and Watson, R. (1986) 'The prediction of small company failure: some behavioural evidence for the UK', *Accounting and Business Research*, Winter, 49–57.

—— (1987) 'Non-financial symptoms and prediction of small company failure: a test of Argenti's hypothesis', *Journal of Business Finance and Accounting*, 14, 3, 335–354.

—— (1992) *Investment and Financing Decisions and the Performance of Small Firms*, A study commissioned by the National Westminster Bank.

Kennedy, H.A. (1975) 'A behavioural study of the usefulness of four financial ratios', *Journal of Accounting Research*, 13, 1, 97–116.

Kets De Vries, M.F.R. (1977) 'The entrepreneurial personality: a person at the crossroads', *Journal of Management Studies*, Feb, 34–57.

—— (1985) 'The dark side of entrepreneurship', *Harvard Business Review*, Nov-Dec, 160–167.

Khan, A.M. (1986) 'Entrepreneur characteristics and the prediction of new venture success, *Omega*, **14**, 5, 365–372.

Lafuente, A. and Salas, V. (1989), 'Types of entrepreneurs and firms: The case of new Spanish firms', *Strategic Management Journal*, **10**, 1, 17–30.

Larson, C.M. and Clute, R.C. (1979) 'The failure syndrome', *American Journal of Small Business*, **4**, 2, 35–43.

Leigh, R., North, D. and Smallbone, D. (1991) 'Adjustment processes in high growth SMEs: a study of mature manufacturing firms in London during the 1980s'. Paper presented at the ESRC Small Business Research Initiative Seminar, University of Warwick 9 Jan.

Lewellen, W.G. and Huntsman, G. (1970) 'Managerial pay and corporate performance', *American Economic Review*, **LX**, 710–720.

Libby, R. (1975) 'Accounting ratios and the prediction of failure: some behavioural evidence', *Journal of Accounting Research*, **13**, 1, 150–162.

Litvak, I.A. and Maule, C.J. (1980) 'Entrepreneurial success or failure – ten years later', *Business Quarterly*, Winter, 68–78.

Lovell, M. (1983) 'Data mining', *The Review of Economics and Statistics*, **65**, 1, 1–11.

Macmillan, I.C. and Day, D.L. (1987) 'Corporate ventures into industrial markets: dynamics of aggressive entry', *Journal of Business Venturing*, **2**, 1, 29–39.

Macmillan Committee (1931) *Report of the Committee on Finance and Industry*, Cmnd 3897, London: HMSO.

Madique, M.A. and Zirger, B.J. (1985) 'The new product learning cycle', *Research Policy*, **14**, 6, 299–313.

Maris, R. (1964) *The Economic Theory of Managerial Capitalism*, London: Macmillan.

Mason, C.M. and Harrison, R.T. (1989) 'The role of the business expansion scheme in the United Kingdom', *Omega*, **17**, 2, 147–157.

—— (1992) 'The supply of equity finance in the UK: a strategy for closing the equity gap', *Entrepreneurship and Regional Development*, **4**, 357–380.

—— (1993) 'Promoting informal venture capital: an evaluation of a British initiative', *Paper presented at the 13th Babson Entrepreneurship Research Conference, University of Babson*.

Mason, C.M., Harrison, R.T. and Chaloner, J. (1991) 'Informal risk capital in the UK: study of investor characteristics, investment preferences and investment decision-making', *Venture Finance Research Project Working Paper No 2*.

Mayer, T. (1975) 'Selecting economic hypotheses by goodness of fit', *The Economic Journal*, **85**, Dec, 877–883.

McClelland, D.C. (1961) *The Achieving Society*, Princeton: N.J.: Van Nostrand.

—— (1986) 'Characteristics of successful entrepreneurs', *The Journal of Creative Behaviour*, **21**, 3, 219–233.

180

McCosker, C.V. (1988) 'Franchising in Australia: trends and outlook', *Management Forum*, 14, 114–122.

McGuire, J.W., Chin, J.S.Y. and Elbing, A.D. (1962) 'Executive income, sales and profits', *American Economic Review*, 52, 753–61.

McMahon, R.G.P., Holmes, S., Hutchinson, P.J. and Forsaith, D.M. (1993) *Small Enterprise Financial Management*, Australia: Harcourt Brace.

Meeks, G. and Whittington, G. (1975) 'Directors' pay, growth and profitability', *Journal of Industrial Economics*, 24, 1–14.

Metcalf, L.E., Frear, C.R. and Krishnan, R. (1992) 'Buyer-seller relationships: an application of the IMP interaction model', *European Journal of Marketing*, 26, 2, 27–46.

Miller, D. and Friesen, P.H. (1982) 'Innovation in conservative and entrepreneurial firms: two models in strategic momentum', *Strategic Management Journal*, 3, 1, 1–25.

Miller, D. and Toulouse, J.M. (1986) 'Chief executive personality and corporate strategy and structure in small firms', *Management Science*, 32, 11, 1389–1409.

Mintzberg, H. (1978) 'Patterns in strategy formation', *Management Science*, 24, 934–948.

—— (1990) 'The design school: reconsidering the basic premises of strategic management', *Strategic Management Journal*, 11, 171–195.

—— and McHugh, A. (1985) 'Strategy formation in an ad hocracy', *Administrative Science Quarterly*, 30, 160–197.

—— and Marris, R. (1966) *The Economic Theory of Managerial Capitalism*, London: Macmillan.

—— and Waters, J.A.(1982) 'Tracking strategy in an entrepreneurial firm', *Academy of Management Journal*, 25, 465–499.

—— (1985) 'Of strategies deliberate and emergent', *Strategic Management Journal*, 6, 257–272.

—— Brunet, J.P. and Waters, J.A. (1986) 'Does planning impede strategic thinking', *Advances in Strategic Management*, 4, Greenwich: JAI Press.

Mueller, D.C. (1972) 'A life cycle theory of the firm', *Journal of Industrial Economics*, 20, 199–219.

North, D., Leigh, R. and Smallbone, D. (1992) 'A comparison of surviving and non-surviving small and medium-sized manufacturing firms in London during the 1980s', *Small Enterprise Development Policy and Practice in Action*, London: Paul Chapman.

OECD (1981) Report of the Committee of Experts on Restrictive Business Practices: *Buyer Power: The Exercise of Market Power by Dominant Buyers*, OECD.

Ohlson, J.A. (1980) 'Financial ratios and the probabilistic prediction of bankruptcy', *Journal of Accounting Research*, 18, 1, 109–132.

Orcutt, G.H. (1948) 'A study of the autoregressive nature of the time series used for Tinbergon's model of the economic system of the United States 1919–32', *Journal of the Royal Statistical Society*, 10.

Orpen, C. (1985) 'The effects of long-range planning on small business performance: a further examination', *Journal of Small Business Management*, 23, 1, 16–23.

Panzar, J. and Willig, R. (1975) 'Economies of scale and economies of scope in multi-product production', Bell Laboratories Discussion Paper No. 33.

Pelham, A.M. and Clayson, D.E. (1988) 'Receptivity to strategic planning tools in small manufacturing firms', *Journal of Small Business Management*, Jan, 43–50.

Perry, C., Meredith, G.C. and Cunnington, H.J. (1988) 'Relationship between small business growth and personal characteristics of owner/managers in Australia', *Journal of Small Business Management*, **26**, **2**, 76–79.

Phillips, B.D. and Kirchhoff, B.A. (1989) 'Formation, growth and survival: small firm dynamics in the US Economy', *Small Business Economics*, **1**, **1**, 65–74.

Porter, M.E. (1980) *Competitive Strategy: Techniques for Analyzing Industries and Competitors*, New York: Free Press.

—— (1985) *Competitive Advantage: Creating and Sustaining Superior Performance*, New York: Free Press.

Randollph, A.W., Sapienza, H.J. and Watson, M.A. (1991) 'Technology-structure fit and performance in small business: an examination of the moderating effects of organizational states', *Entrepreneurship: Theory and Practice*, Autumn, 27–40.

Ray, G. and Hutchinson, P.J. (1985) *The Financing and Financial Control of Small Enterprise Development*, London: Gower.

Reid, G.C. (1993) *Small Business Enterprise*, London: Routledge.

Rice, G.H. Jnr, and Lindecamp, D.P. (1989) 'Personality types and business success of small retailers', *Journal of Occupational Psychology*, **62**, 2, 177–182.

Roberts, E.B. (1959) *Executive Compensation*, Glencoe, IL: Free Press.

Robinson, R.B. Jnr, (1982) 'The importance of "outsiders" in small firm strategic planning', *Academy of Management Journal*, **25**, 1, 80–93.

—— (1983) 'Measures of small firm effectiveness for strategic planning research', *Journal of Small Business Management*, **21**, 2, 22–29.

—— and Pearce II, J.A. (1983) 'The impact of formalized planning on financial performance in small organizations', *Strategic Management Journal*, **4**, 197–207.

—— (1984) 'Research thrusts in small firm strategic planning', *Academy of Management Review*, 9, 1, 128–137

—— (1988) 'Planned patterns of strategic behaviour and their relationship to business unit performance', *Strategic Management Journal*, **9**, 43–60.

—— Salem, M., Logan, J.E. and Pearce, J.A. II (1986) 'Planning activities related to independent retail firm performance', *American Journal of Small Business*, 11, 1, 19–26.

Rothwell R., Freeman C., Horsley, A., Jervis, V.T.P., Robertson, A.B. and Townsend, J. (1974) 'Project Sappho updated: project phase II', *Research Policy* 3, 3, 258–291.

Routamaa, V. and Vesalainen, J. (1987) 'Types of entrepreneurship and strategic level goal setting', *International Small Business Journal*, 5, 3, 19–29.

Sandberg, W.R. and Hofer, C.W. (1987) 'Improving new venture performance: the role of strategy, industry structure and the entrepreneur', *Journal of Business Venturing*, 2, 1, 5–28.

Scarborough., N.M. and Zimmer, T.W. (1987) 'Strategic planning for the small business', *Business*, 2, 2, 11–19.

Schwenk, C.R. and Shrader, C.B. (1993) 'The effects of formal strategic planning on financial performance in small firms: a meta analysis', *Entrepreneurship Theory and Practise*, 17, 3, 53–64.

Shrader, C.B., Mulford, C.L. and Blackburn, V.L. (1989) 'Strategic and operational planning, uncertainty and performance in small firms', *Journal of Small Business Management*, 27, 4, 45–60.

Shuman, J.C. (1975) 'Corporate planning in small companies – a survey', *Long Range Planning*, October, 81–90.

—— Shaw, J.J. and Sussman, G. (1985) 'Strategic planning in smaller rapid growth companies', *Long Range Planning*, 18, 6, 48–55.

Simmons, P. (1989) 'Bad luck and fixed costs in personal bankruptcies', *Economic Journal*, 99, 92–107.

Small Business Research Trust 'Small Business Finance', *Nat West Quarterly Survey of Small Business in Britain'*, 7, 4, 19–21.

Smallbone, D., North, D. and Leigh, R. (1993) 'Strategies for high growth SMEs in the 1980s'. Paper presented at a conference on 'The Development of Strategies of SMEs in the 1990s', Helsinki.

Smith, N.R. (1967) *The Entrepreneur and the Firm: The Relationship Between Type of Man and Type of Company*, Bureau of Business and Economic Research, Michigan State University, East Lansing: Michigan.

Smith, N.R. and Miner, J.B. (1983) 'Type of entrepreneur, type of firm and managerial motivation: implications for organizational lifecycle theory', *Strategic Management Journal*, 4, 325–340.

Smyth, D., Boyles, W.J. and Peseau, D.E. (1975) *Size Growth Profits and Executive Compensation in the Large Corporation*, London: Macmillan.

Stanworth, M.J.K. and Curran, J. (1976) 'Growth and the small firm – an alternative view', *Journal of Management Studies*, 13, 2, 95–110.

Stanworth, J., Blyth, S., Granger, B. and Stanworth, C. (1989) 'Who becomes an entrepreneur?', *International Small Business Journal*, 8, 1, 11–22 .

Steiner, M.P. and Solem, O. (1988) 'Factors for success in small manufacturing firms', *Journal of Small Business Management*, 26, 1, 51–56.

Stiglitz, J.E. and Weiss, A. (1981) ' Credit rationing in markets with imperfect competition', *American Economic Review*, 71, 3, 393–410.

Storey D. and Strange, A. (1992) 'Entrepreneurship in Cleveland 1979–1989. A study of the effects of the enterprise culture', *Department of Employment Research Series No 3*.

—— Keasey K., Watson R. and Wynarczk P. (1987) *The Performance of Small Firms*, London: Croom Helm.

—— Watson R. and Wynarczk P. (1989) 'Fast growth small businesses', *Department of Employment Research Paper No. 67*.

—— Watson, R. and Wynarczyk, P. 'Fast growth small businesses. Case studies of 40 small firms in north-east England', *Department of Employment Research Paper*, No 67.

Stratos Group (1990) *Strategic Orientation of Small European Business*. Aldershot: Avebury-Gower.

Stuart, R. and Abetti, P.A. (1987) 'Start-up ventures: towards the prediction of initial success', *Journal of Business Venturing*, **2**, 215–230.

Taffler, R. J. (1982) 'Forecasting company failure in the UK using discriminant analysis and financial ratio data', *Journal of the Royal Statistical Society*, (A) **1.45**, part 3, 342–358.

—— (1983) 'Empirical models for the monitoring of UK corporations: the state of the art', *City University Business School Working Paper, Series No. 51*.

Taylor, B., Gilinsky, A., Hilmi, A., Haln, D. and Grab, U. (1990) 'Strategy and leadership in growth companies', *Long Range Planning*, **23**, 3, 66–75.

Teece, D.J. (1980) 'Economies of scale and the scope of the enterprise', *Journal of Economic Behaviour and Organisation*, 223–247.

Van Horne, J.C. (1976) 'Optimal initiation, **31**, 897–911.

Vesper, K.H. (1990) *New Venture Strategies*, New Jersey: Prentice Hall.

Von Hippel, E.A. (1976) 'The dominant role of users in the scientific instrumentation innovation process', *Research Policy*, **5**, 212–239.

—— (1977) 'Transferring process equipment innovations from user–innovators to equipment manufacturing firms', *R and D Management*, **8**, 1, 13–22.

Wadhwani, B. (1986) 'Inflation, bankruptcy, default premia and the stock market', *Economic Journal*, **96**, 120–138.

Watson, R. (1990) 'Employment change, profits and directors' remuneration in small and closely held UK companies', *Scottish Journal of Political Economy*, **37**, 3, 259–273.

Welsh, J.A. and White, J.F. (1981) 'A small business is not a little big business', *Harvard Business Review*, July-August, 18–32.

Wetzel, W.E. (1986a) 'Entrepreneurs, angels and economic renaissance', in Hisnch, R.D. (ed.) *Entrepreneurship, Intrapreneurship and Venture Capital*, Lexington, MA: Lexington Books, 119–139.

—— (1986b) 'Informal risk capital: knowns and unknowns' in Sexton, D.L. and Sunil, R.W. (eds) *The Art and Science of Entrepreneurship*, Cambridge, MA: Ballinger, 85–108.

White, M.J. (1989) 'The corporate bankruptcy decision', *Journal of Economic Perspectives*, **3**, 2, 129–151.

Wilson, D.T., Hansang-Lin and Holler, G.W. (1989) *Research in Marketing: An International Perspective*, IMP 5th Conference, Institute for the Study of Business Markets: The Pennsylvania State University.

Wilson, H. (1974) *The Financing of Small Firms*: Report of the Committee to Review the Functioning of Financial Institutions (Cmnd 7503) London: HMSO.

Womack, J.P., Jones, D.T and Roos, D. (1990) *The Machine that Changed the World*, New York: Macmillan.

Wood, D. and Piesse, J. (1988), 'The information value of failure predictions in credit assessment', *Journal of Banking and Finance*, **12**, 2, 275–292.

Zavgren, C.V. (1983) 'The prediction of failure: the state of the art', *Journal of Accounting Literature* (Spring).

Zimmer, I. (1986) 'A lens study of the prediction of corporate failure by bank loan officers', *Journal of Accounting Research*, **18**, 2, 629–636.

INDEX

185